PRAISE FOR #HOOKED

'Transplanting an idea is a little like transplanting a human organ: the natural human response is to reject it. Patrick Fagan's book gives you access to the psychological equivalent of immuno-suppressants - the creative techniques and stories which allow a new idea or message to avoid automatic rejection.'
Rory Sutherland, Vice Chairman, Ogilvy & Mather

'This book is essential reading for anyone wanting to bridge the gap between the science and practice of influence. Packed with original, yet evidence-based, suggestions, it digests the core findings of behavioural economics and psychology to help readers make smarter decisions and increase their impact on others. Highly recommended!'
Tomas Chamorro-Premuzic, Professor of Business Psychology at UCL and Columbia University, and CEO of Hogan Assessments

'From bizarre psychological principles to testing approaches that actually work, this book is a must-read for anyone wishing to understand the science behind persuasive messages.'
Nathalie Nahai, web psychologist and author

'Warning! Learnings from science will make your communications more effective. Patrick makes the science accessible and shows how to apply it pragmatically. A must-read for marketers and agencies.'
Phil Barden, author of *Decoded: The Science Behind Why We Buy*

'Want more people to listen to what you have to say? This book provides a handy toolkit to make anyone a better communicator.'
Jonah Berger, Wharton Professor and bestselling author of *Contagious: Why Things Catch On*

#HOOKED

#HOOKED

Why cute sells ... and other marketing magic that we just can't resist

PATRICK FAGAN

PEARSON

Harlow, England • London • New York • Boston • San Francisco • Toronto • Sydney
Auckland • Singapore • Hong Kong • Tokyo • Seoul • Taipei • New Delhi
Cape Town • São Paulo • Mexico City • Madrid • Amsterdam • Munich • Paris • Milan

PEARSON EDUCATION LIMITED

Edinburgh Gate
Harlow CM20 2JE
United Kingdom
Tel: +44 (0)1279 623623
Web: www.pearson.com/uk

First published 2016 (print and electronic)

ISBN: 978–1–292–07442–9 (print)
    978–1–292–07444–3 (PDF)
    978–1–292–07445–0 (ePub)

British Library Cataloguing-in-Publication Data
A catalogue record for the print edition is available from the British Library

Library of Congress Cataloging-in-Publication Data
A catalog record for the print edition is available from the Library of Congress

10 9 8 7 6 5 4 3 2 1
20 19 18 17 16

Cover design by Two Associates
Dog image © Eric Isselee/Shutterstock.com
Hook and paper image © fikmik/123rf.com
Print edition typeset in 9.5/13.75 Helvetica Neue LT W1G by SPi Global
Print edition printed in Malaysia (CTP–PJB)

NOTE THAT ANY PAGE CROSS REFERENCES REFER TO THE PRINT EDITION

CONTENTS

PART 1 AN INTRODUCTION

PART 2 SECTION 1 INVITE ATTENTION

SECTION 2 IGNITE THINKING

SECTION 3 INCITE ACTION

PART 3 PUTTING IT TO USE

NOTE

This book is so scientific that the references list – at almost 20,000 words – is too large to include! To view the citations, please go to:

http://www.brainchimp.co.uk/hooked/notes

ABOUT THE AUTHOR

Patrick Fagan is a consumer psychologist with both academic and commercial credentials. He is currently an Associate Lecturer in Consumer Behaviour and Psychology of Marketing and Advertising at Goldsmiths, University of London, and a Lecturer in Consumer Psychology at London College of Fashion, University of the Arts London. He has published a number of papers on topics ranging from price psychology to Facebook psychology, and has written for publications including *The Guardian, AdMap* and *Psychology Today.* He is a frequent media contributor on consumer psychology and has been interviewed for print, radio and TV by companies like the BBC, *Evening Standard* and *London Live.*

Commercially, Patrick has been applying behavioural science to commercial insights for over five years, both as an employee for agencies and on an independent basis. He currently works for CrowdEmotion, a company pioneering multi-signal emotional capture and its meaningful application in the real world; his consultancy brainchimp.co.uk has conducted controlled psychological experiments, contributed to press releases and provided consultancy for brands including eBay, RealD and Vodafone.

You can reach Patrick at oohooh@brainchimp.co.uk

THANKS AND ACKNOWLEDGEMENTS

Thanks to all who contributed to this book.

First and foremost, thanks to D. Many further thanks to Thomas Bayne and the rest of Mountainview Learning, who introduced me to some of the great case studies in this book, and to the business brain science way of thinking. To find out if you could benefit from Mountainview's fantastic brain science insights, visit http://mountainview.co.uk/assumptions-quiz/

Thank you Nathalie for your support. Likewise, thank you Adrian, Dimitros, Gorkan and Tomas at UCL.

And thank you to Eloise and her colleagues at Pearson for all of their hard work on the book.

PUBLISHER'S ACKNOWLEDGEMENTS

We are grateful to the following for permission to reproduce copyright material:

Photos

Photo on pxi © Liliya Kulianionak/Shutterstock.com; photos on p12 © R. Gino Santa Maria/Shutterstock.com (woman with rose) and © John Foxx Collection/Imagestate (man with sunglasses); photos on p28 © 123rf.com (spider, rock and rose) and © Andrey Starostin (mushroom); photo on p38 © Richard Levine/Alamy Stock Photo; photo on p40 © Eric Isselee/Shutterstock.com; photo on p42 © Simon_g; photo on p48 © Jack Hinds/Alamy Stock Photo; photo on p53 © David Pearson/Alamy Stock Photo; photo on p61 © Guy Bell/ Alamy Stock Photo; photo on p63 © USBFCO/Shutterstock.com; photo on p68 'Monkey Sparrow' by Sarah DeRemer; photo on p70 © Ana Blazic Lav-lovic; photo on p71 © Justin Kase Zninez/Alamy Stock Photo; photos on p76 from Sajjacholapunt, P. and Ball, L. J., 'The influence of banner adverstise-ments on attention and memory: human faces with averted gaze can enhance advertising effectiveness', *Frontiers in Psychology*, 5, 166, 2014; photo on p112 © razorpix/Alamy Stock Photo; photo on p123 © Chris Howes/Wild Places

Photography/Alamy Stock Photo; photo on p124 © Krsmanovic; photos on p144 © Baloncici (cushion), © Joe Gough (dinner plate), © Horiyan (table), © DJ Srki (chair) and © Joey Chan/Pearson Education Asia Ltd (stool); photo on p155 © Newscast-online Limited/Alamy Stock Photo.

Figures

Figure on p14 adapted from Lavidge, R. J and Steiner, G. A. (1961). 'A model for predictive measures of advertising effectiveness', *Journal of Marketing*, 25, 59–62; figure on p22 © 123rf.com; figure on p82 adapted from Huron, D., *Sweet Anticipation: Music and the Psychology of Expectation*, MIT Press, 206; figure on p90 adapted from Johnson, E. J. and Goldstein, D. G. (2003). 'Do defaults save lives?', *Science,* 302, 1338–1339.

LET'S GET #HOOKED

Source: © Liliya Kulianionak/Shutterstock.com

Take a good look at this puppy.

Thanks to Mr Figglesnuff, you'll pay closer attention to everything you're about to read; researchers have actually shown that pictures of cute animals make people more attentive.[1]

It's bizarre and counterintuitive, but science suggests it's true – and that's the point. When it comes to communicating effectively – that is, making sticky messages that *get people hooked* (and 'messages' in this book refer to corporate communications including advertising, branding, direct mail, emails, social media posts, editorial content and pitches and presentations) – a lot of businesspeople are scrambling around in the dark and taking their best guesses; often what they believe is right is wrong, and what they believe is wrong is right.

Take the American insurance company Aflac.[2] In 2003 the CEO, Daniel P. Amos, had a strange idea for a new ad campaign: a duck that quacked the brand name 'Aflac'. That was it.

Nobody at the company expected it to work – why would it?

Amos recalled:

> *When I tried explaining to people what we were thinking about, no one got it. 'Well, there's this duck', I'd say. 'And he quacks Aflac'. The response was always the same: a silent stare. So I stopped telling people. I didn't even tell our board; I just said we were trying something very bold and creative for our advertising campaign.*

Just like the Aflac executives, you probably wouldn't think that a bizarre, semi-sentient duck would work, that it could actually influence people and help the business; but it did. Amos reported the campaign helped to drive up revenues by 44% over the following seven years.

So, how *do* messages work – and how *don't* they work – and what does psychology tell us about it?

Well, read on, dear reader, and find out! In the meantime though, an interesting experiment will serve as an introductory appetiser.

The study in question investigated urban legends.[3] Have you heard the one about the man who bought a McDonald's chicken burger, only to bite into a fat, juicy *tumour*? What about the one that says if chocolate makes you sneeze, it's because of all the crushed up insects that fall into it during production? (That one appears to be true[4] – sorry!)

These examples give you a clue as to what kinds of urban legends are the stickiest. The researchers asked participants to read some popular urban legends and rate them on a range of factors, such as the elicitation of emotions and how likely they would be to pass the story on. The chart below shows the predictive power of various factors for the pass-along variable.

Predictive power for sharing

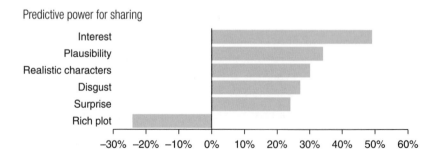

This experiment emphasises the importance to stickiness of emotion (disgust), surprise, curiosity (interest), narrative (realistic characters) and fluency (a simple plot). These are just five of the ten psychological principles of getting your messages hooked in this book:

1 **Primal** Our 'chimp brains' still have a huge effect on what we pay attention to; for example, it's not very sexy to say so, but sex does sell.

2 **Affective** We all have first-hand experience with the attention-grabbing power of emotion – most of us have wasted hours online looking at videos of kittens and puppies.

3 **Self-relevant** Imagine you're walking down the street, and a stranger walks past wearing a T-shirt with a picture of your face on it; you would notice it immediately.

4 **Surprising** When a waiter drops a tray of plates onto the floor, most everyone will look (some will even applaud). It's in our nature to pay attention to anything surprising.

5 **Mystery** A whole industry of crosswords, codewords and sudokus speaks to our innate desire to 'close the gaps' in our understanding and solve mysteries.

6 **Ease** People generally have little time and motivation to attend to messages – but mostly, people are just lazy. Which do you take more often, the escalator or the stairs?

7 **Narrative** As a species, we have been structuring and sharing information using narrative for eons – stories are part of our collective psyche; stories are relatable.

8 **Memory** There is typically a long break between the time a message is read and the time it's meant to have an effect on behaviour – so it's vital that it's remembered.

9 **Autopilot** We have very limited brainpower, so we use non-conscious shortcuts or rules-of-thumb – called *heuristics* – to guide our behaviour. These can be 'hotwired' via a message.

10 **Priming** Don't think of a white bear. You will have invariably thought of a white bear. Priming is influencing behaviour by bringing certain ideas to the front of people's minds.

With these insights, your messages will be seen, and your voice will be heard!

PART 1

AN INTRODUCTION

CHALLENGING ASSUMPTIONS WITH EXAMPLES

> *" HeadOn: Apply directly to the forehead! HeadOn: Apply directly to the forehead! HeadOn: Apply directly to the forehead!*

So goes perhaps one of the worst adverts of all time. HeadOn is a chapstick-like product that, the brand claims, can be rubbed onto the forehead to relieve headaches; unsurprisingly, there is no actual proof that it works (see http://abcnews.go.com/GMA/Health/story?id=2695490).[1] Accordingly, the brand was perhaps a little limited in what it could say in its advertising, and ended up with the very simple and literal copy you see quoted above.

It was basic and irritating, but guess what? It worked. Sales increased by 234% year on year after the ad's launch.[2]

Let's take another example. Most British readers will be all too familiar with the price comparison site GoCompare.com – or more specifically, its infuriating tenor mascot Gio Compario. For those lucky enough to be unaware, in 2009 the brand released an advert featuring a portly opera singer wearing a tuxedo and sporting a ridiculous curtains haircut and an even more ridiculous twirly moustache, and singing an *extremely* catchy song.[3]

The advert was weird, it was unique, and it was *hated.* It was so despised and detested, in fact, that it was named the most irritating ad of the year in 2009[4] – *and* 2010![5] It was hated *so* much that the brand followed up with a campaign in which the tenor was killed by various means, including a bazooka; eventually, in 2014, the brand dropped him altogether.[6] The brand's Marketing Officer, Kevin Hughes, said, 'It was risky, but a brand has to listen to its customers'.[7]

But does it?

It seems intuitive that the mascot should be dropped – customers did hate it, after all. But intuitions and assumptions can often be wrong; what really matters is the evidence.

Within three months of originally introducing the advert, GoCompare saw an increase in customer count by 20%, quote volumes by 44%, and brand awareness by a massive 450%.[8] In other words, it *worked.* Dropping the mascot may have been a mistake, and one based on false assumptions about how communication works (although it's too early to tell from the data).

Examples like these highlight the need to take a fresh look at how communication works, and to challenge old ways of thinking.

FOOLED BY RANDOMNESS

Clever Hans was a horse – a clever horse, by all accounts.[9] At the start of the twentieth century, Hans toured Germany with his owner Wilhelm von Osten, and performed a range of amazing tricks for the crowds who gathered to see him; Hans was capable of mathematical feats that would stump even some humans. For example, von Osten would ask Hans a mathematical sum, and Hans would tap the answer out with his hoof. Unfortunately, though, it was too good to be true: believe it or not, horses are generally *not* capable of maths. An investigation discovered that Hans would tap his foot and stop after his owner's involuntary and almost imperceptible body language gave him the cue to do so – a tasty treat for the right answer conditioned this response.

However, the case of Clever Hans raises a clever point. All animals are hardwired to spot patterns in the environment; if they did not, they would not discover, for example, that certain berries are poisonous.

From horses to humans, many experiments have long-since illustrated that we innately detect patterns. For example, studies have shown that people are able to guess the outcome from a sequence of cards with a certain pattern, even if they cannot consciously describe that pattern or explain how they guessed the next card correctly.[10]

This phenomenon can have its downsides. We sometimes spot patterns where they do not actually exist – what is known as *apophena*.[11]

In *Fooled by Randomness*,[12] Nassim Taleb explains:

> *. . . we are not made to view things as independent from each other. When viewing two events A and B, it is hard not to assume that A causes B, B causes A, or both cause each other. Our bias is immediately to establish a causal link.*

SEEING PATTERNS THAT DON'T EXIST

Do you have £200 to spare? Why not visit GhostStop.com and pick up a Zoom 360° EVP Recorder to pick up the sounds of ghosts speaking their spooky messages?[13] Simply head over to a haunted house and record the silence, and when you play the recording turn it up to maximum volume so you can hear the spooky spectral whisperings among the static.

Well, because ghosts' voices do not exist: they are simply an example of people finding patterns that aren't actually there.[14] Other examples include pareidolia, where we see faces such as 'the man in the moon',[15] and the 'hot hand' fallacy, where gamblers believe they are on a winning streak and bet accordingly, rather than at the mercy of chance.[16]

The point of all this is that many of us believe in our own patterns that may not actually be true, and they can affect the power of our messages; it is vital to be *scientific.*

For example, you probably believe that messages spelling out the dangers of cigarettes will help stop people from smoking. In actual fact, research shows that anti-smoking messages can have the *opposite* effect, because the message makes the idea of smoking mentally salient and tempts people to do it.[17]

We are living in what advertising executive Bob Hoffman calls 'The Golden Age of Bullshit':[19] the message-makers of our day, particularly marketers and advertisers, are full of nonsense. Their ideas of what works are based on decades of theory, creative thinking and brainstorming – but very little evidence.

ACTION POINT

Imagine you work as Communications Manager at a grocery supermarket in the aftermath of the 'horsemeat scandal', when many of the store's meat products were found to contain horsemeat (when they were not supposed to).

Craft a Tweet (maximum 140 characters) to send from the brand's Twitter account in response to the scandal.

Now spend five minutes thinking about why you wrote that Tweet. What was your intended aim and how did you go about achieving it? What principles were behind your thinking? Where did those principles come from? Are you sure they are correct? What is the scientific evidence for them?

In *The 7 Habits of Highly Effective People*, Steven Covey outlines the 'See, Do, Get' model shown below.[18] While many people spend time on 'Do' (i.e. putting their beliefs into action), and 'Get' (i.e. reviewing and interpreting the results of their actions), very few spend time on 'See' – in other words, Covey states that few people spend time thinking about and challenging their underlying beliefs, and that doing so is an important factor for success.

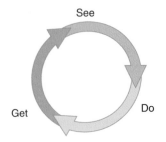

The authors of one paper went through the top marketing textbooks at the time and found hundreds and hundreds of instructions – but guess how many were supported by evidence?[20]

Zero.

Hoffman wrote:[21]

 Medical practitioners, who were trained in the practice of bloodletting, never questioned its efficacy. They just assumed it worked because they were taught it worked and they credulously attributed the fact that some people got well to the treatment . . . We are faced with a similar problem today . . . For almost 20 years, advertising programs, marketing courses, and professional development classes have taught these people principles that can now be labelled either seriously flawed or outright baloney . . . never before in my experience has a whole generation of marketing and advertising people been taught an entire set of principles that is so lacking in a factual basis, and so influenced by anecdotes and fantasies.

It's hardly surprising, then, that surveys by consultancy The Fournaise Group found that 70% of CEOs have lost trust in marketers' ability to deliver tangible business results,[22] or that big brands around the world are slashing their marketing departments.[23]

The truth is that most professional and business messages just don't work. They're based on misinformation and hunches – and bad hunches, at that.

How about you – what are your beliefs when it comes to messages that work? Try yourself on the quiz below.

Belief	True	False
A message must change attitudes in order to change behaviour		
People have to like a message or its sender for it to work		
Most of the time, responses to messages are well thought out		
People consciously decide which messages to pay attention to		
A message has to be processed consciously for it to have an effect		
A message must be persuasive in order to have an effect		
The most effective messages contain rational information		
It's more effective if a person reads a message than thinks it in their heads		
The more information in a message, the better		
Negative emotions should be avoided in messages		

If you answered that any of the statements are true, then you may not be communicating messages as effectively as you could be.

So what does the *science* say?

1 THE SCIENCE OF COMMUNICATION

Imagine, if you will, that you are a chimp. You are monkeying around in Tanzania, when suddenly you come across a tasty-smelling fruit that's entirely new to you, and you can't seem to get the nut open to access the juicy flesh inside. One of your troop, however, knows what to do, and cracks and twists the fruit in such a way that opens it.

You try to do the same thing and it doesn't work straight away; what do you do? Do you: (a) keep trying to open it the way your chimp friend did; or (b) give up on that and try to figure it out yourself?

As a human, you probably went with option (a), following the lead of a peer; an actual chimp, meanwhile, would have gone with option (b).

Vicky Horner and Andrew Whiten published the results of an experiment in 2005 that looked at this very question.[1] They performed an experiment with both chimpanzees and human children, in which the participants were shown a technique to open a puzzle box in order to get to the tasty treat inside. However, in some cases the participants were tricked and shown a method to open the box that didn't actually succeed, although it appeared to when the researcher did it.

The researchers found that the human children would persist with what they had seen others do, while the chimps quickly ignored it and did their own thing; the conclusion being that humans are uniquely social learners.

Importantly, primatologists have found that humans and primates share several cognitive biases. For example, researchers at Yale University managed to teach capuchin monkeys the value of money over a period of several months by giving them round discs and teaching them that the discs could be exchanged for food.[2] The monkeys exhibited financial behaviours also seen in humans. For one, the discs were observed being exchanged by the monkeys for sex (it really *is* the oldest profession in the world); but also, the monkeys exhibited cognitive biases like loss aversion, where an object's selling price is higher than its buying price due to an innate fear of loss. Likewise, while people will insult their co-workers and slack off if they feel they are being treated unfairly by their employer,[3] a capuchin monkey will throw its cucumber treat back in its handler's face if it sees another monkey being given tasty grapes instead.[4]

On the other hand, taking our cues from the messages of others is a uniquely human bias. In addition to Horner and Whiten's study, another illustration comes from research showing that pointing is something unique to humans – chimpanzees only learn to point when they are in captivity.[5] Human infants, meanwhile, will learn to point and gesture with social meaning within the first 12 months of their lives.[6]

SOCIAL COGNITION

The massive influence of social information on human behaviour is illustrated by a wealth of case studies from the field of social cognition.

Perhaps the most famous is Kitty Genovese.[7] The story goes like this . . . Catherine 'Kitty' Genovese was an attractive 28-year-old woman who was stabbed to death near her home in Queens, New York, one evening in 1964. The important detail is that Kitty allegedly screamed for help, and although dozens of people living nearby heard her cries, none called the emergency services. The principle believed to be at play was 'the diffusion of responsibility' – people felt less responsibility to help since they believed others would do so instead.

Recent investigations suggest that the Kitty Genovese example may be rather apocryphal;[8] however, psychological experiments since then have supported the principle. One fantastic piece of research involved participants left sitting in a room to await the start of the experiment;[9] as they were waiting, smoke was released into the room through a vent. The subject was either sitting in the room on their own, or sitting with two other people who were in fact actors instructed to ignore the smoke and do nothing. On their own, three-quarters of participants left the room and sought help; in the presence of passive others, only one in ten did so.

When it comes to messages that work, there are two important implications from the points made previously. Firstly – and as we'll cover in more detail later in the book – messages can be made more effective through understanding social biases.

MAKING MESSAGES SOCIAL

Have you, for example, ever sent an important request around the office via email, and copied in all of your colleagues? Maybe you were asking people to donate to your Just Giving marathon page; or perhaps you were asking for volunteers. Whatever your aim, you could have had more luck.

Liberal use of the CC field should generally be avoided when making requests via email. This is not just because of the potential for awful social gaffes – as the manager of a Massachusetts Five Guys restaurant who accidentally copied a customer in on an email calling him a 'douche' will tell you.[10] (http://www.dailymail .co.uk/news/article-2564086/Five-Guys-manager-accidentally-includes-customer-email-calling-douche.html) – but also because of diffusion of responsibility.

To illustrate, students at one university were sent an email from a fellow student with the subject line 'Please Help' and a message asking if the university had a biology faculty. The email was either sent to a recipient directly, or else to the recipient and another four students. Among those emailed directly, 64% replied, compared to 50% of those emailed as part of a group.[11]

So, messages are their most effective when they take social principles into account.

WHY MESSAGES MATTER

The second point, more broadly, is that sending messages is an important part of who we are as a species – and as such, it's vital we get it right.

The desire to communicate effectively has been a driving force behind some of our greatest accomplishments. William Henry Fox Talbot was a British inventor who pioneered highly influential photography techniques which are in use to this day.[12] In 1833, Talbot was on holiday at Lake Como in Italy; he was so taken with the scenery that he sketched it in the hope that he could share it with friends and family back home. Try as he might, however, he simply could not capture the beauty of the scene in his sketchbook, and he was inspired to create a machine that could sketch a scene accurately enough to share it with others.

Fast forward almost two hundred years to the present day. The latest statistics from Facebook state that 830 million people use it daily.[13] Talbot's urge to share Lake Como with his friends and family has developed into Facebook, Instagram, Vine, *et al.* Messages are a bigger part of our lives than ever.

Since the start of the decade, global internet penetration has increased by an estimated 760%, such that 40% of the world's population (that's three billion people) now have internet access.[14] By 2018, it is predicted that there will be 83,299 petabytes (that's 83,299 quadrillion bytes) of internet traffic every month;[14] in concrete terms, that is the equivalent of about 34 trillion MP3s.[15]

In 2010 alone, Google CEO Eric Schmidt said, 'There were 5 exabytes of information created between the dawn of civilization through 2003, but that much information is now created every 2 days.'[16]

So, not only is there an innate, evolutionary urge to communicate well, but technological forces mean that ineffective messages will simply get lost in the noise. Every day, on average, people receive 88 emails,[17] spend 40 minutes on Facebook,[18] and are exposed to up to 3,500 advertisements.[19] There is an increasing amount of static through which businesses' messages have to cut: if they don't, they will simply be a waste of time and money.

So, how *do* you create messages which work? Let's start with the accepted view.

TRADITIONAL APPROACHES TO GETTING READ

Perhaps the most well-known model of effective communication is the elaboration-likelihood model of persuasion, from Richard Petty and John Cacioppo.[20] The model essentially states that communications are variably effective at changing attitudes according to whether they use information in line with how the receiver is processing the message.

If the message is processed through the *central* route, the receiver puts a lot of conscious, deliberative thought (i.e. elaboration) into it; in which case, the message should present rational information. For example, in this case, a toilet paper brand (let's call it Snuffles) putting out a press release about the fluffiness and absorbance of its tissues might discuss how they performed in controlled trials at mopping up oil and cola and the like. However, if the message is processed through the *peripheral* route, the receiver puts little thought (elaboration) into it, and the message should present subtle cues. In this instance, the Snuffles brand might hint at fluffiness and absorption through the image of, say, a labrador puppy.

The central route to persuasion	The peripheral route to persuasion
The audience takes a direct and outright (or central) approach to the information in a message. Here, explicit information is most useful – it will be processed consciously.	The audience takes a subtle and roundabout (or peripheral) approach to information. In this case, implicit or sensory information is most useful – it will be processed non-consciously.

The model proposes that consumers process the message centrally or peripherally according to motivation – putting more thought into a leaflet about organ donation than, say, buying Girl Scout cookies – and ability – such as intelligence or lack of distractions.

However, there are ostensibly three issues with this model, and the many others like it in the communications literature.

The first potential problem is that this model focuses on attitude change as paramount. The assumption behind this model, and more explicitly championed in Azjen's theory of planned behaviour,[21] is that changing attitudes will lead to a change in behaviour.

But is this certainly the case?

SAY VERSUS DO

Going back to HeadOn and GoCompare, it seems irrelevant to an advert's success whether consumers have a positive or negative attitude towards it. In fact, a large-scale review of advertising research found that the more an advert was repeated, the worse consumers' attitudes became towards it – but that sales were maintained or even increased in line with repetition![22]

In 1934, Richard LaPiere conducted a seminal study which questioned the assumed attitude–behaviour relationship.[23] LaPiere travelled around 1930s America with his student and his student's wife, both of whom were Chinese; the three patronised several hotels, motels and restaurants, only one of which (out of 251) refused them service. Later, LaPiere sent a survey to all of the establishments asking, 'Will you accept members of the Chinese race in your establishment?'

Among those who responded, over nine in ten said they would refuse service to Chinese customers. The results were seen as evidence that behaviours are often very different from attitudes.

Of course, there were a number of concerns with LaPiere's methodology (the Chinese couple were accompanied by a white professor in person, after all), but more recent studies have supported the general principle. For example, an experiment in 2012 asked a group of students to rate how admirable they found a course of action to be compared to inaction; action was seen as significantly more favourable. However, when asked if they would rather take their exams soon, or put them off, significantly more of the students opted for the latter. The researchers titled their paper 'Do as I say (not as I do)'.[24]

More explicitly, an early review of research found that the average correlation between attitudes and behaviours was rarely above 0.30, and often nearer to 0, with the researcher stating, 'It is considerably more likely that attitudes will be unrelated or only slightly related to overt behaviours.'[25]

More recent reviews have been more positive, finding average correlations of 0.38 in 1995[26] and 0.52 in 2006[27] – but this is still far from a 1:1 relationship.

The reason for this is that people generally have very little awareness of the subconscious drivers of their behaviour, and instead produce so-called 'naïve theories' to post-rationalise or predict their actions. As behavioural scientist Colin Camerer put it, 'The human brain is like a monkey brain with a cortical "press secretary" who is glib at concocting explanations for behaviour, and who privileges deliberative explanations over cruder ones.'[28]

A seminal study conducted by Benjamin Libet and colleagues frankly suggested that free will is an illusion.[29] To put it simply, in the experiment participants were asked to push a button at their leisure, and to indicate when they had decided to push it. An EEG cap recorded each participant's brain activity in order to measure when the brain had set the button-push action in motion.

And the time lag between deciding to push the button, and the brain initiating the action? It was −350ms on average. In other words, the brain had initiated the button-push before the participant 'decided' to do it – the implication being that our 'decisions' are actually post-rationalisations. Attitudes can be poor predictors of behaviour because they don't determine actions, but are actually interpretations of them.

Not only that, in fact, but it might actually be the case that behaviours drive attitudes, rather than attitudes driving behaviours. In a fascinating experiment on a principle called *the facial feedback hypothesis,* participants were asked to hold a pen in their mouths – some were asked to hold it in

Illustration of difference between holding a pen in the teeth, like a rose, or mouth, like a cigarette

Sources: © R. Gino Santa Maria/Shutterstock.com (woman with rose); © John Foxx Collection/Imagestate (man with sunglasses)

their teeth, like a rose, and the others in their mouth, like a cigarette. They then watched some cartoons and rated them in terms of funniness. Those made to smile by the pen rated the cartoons as funnier: in this experiment, the behaviour (smiling) drove the attitude (a positive perception of the cartoons).[30]

Average cartoon funniness rating

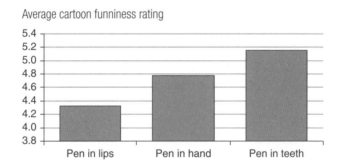

Another great study to illustrate this point asked participants to fill out a survey on a clipboard to indicate their personal opinions on Israel and Palestine. When participants flipped the sheet to answer the rest of the survey, a sneaky adhesive patch on the back of the clipboard peeled away the participant's original answers, leaving responses which completely opposed their actual beliefs. Then, the participants were asked to explain their answers. Over half (53%) did not notice any change and consequently argued in favour of opinions they did not actually give.[31]

The takeaway is that attitudes are often poor predictors of behaviour; if the goal of a message is to change behaviour, it is far more effective to do that directly through psychological principles.

'THE CHIMP BRAIN': PREPARE FOR IRRATIONALITY

A similar, second issue with the aforementioned model is that it places almost too much emphasis on the rational side of an audience. As will be discussed, only a minority of cognitive processing is conscious.[32] The model claims that people will use the peripheral processing route for messages when motivation is high, yet studies have found that subtle, non-conscious principles have significant effects when people read letters offering expensive pay-day loans,[33] when people respond to pension plans,[34] and even when doctors decide which medicine to prescribe a patient.[35]

In fact, research has shown that advertising messages, for example, are the most effective when they are entirely emotional and contain little or no rational content at all.[36] It appears that the best messages, therefore, may be those that neglect the rational side of decision-making entirely; at least, to weight the two systems equally is likely a mistake.

The third and final problem is that the model ostensibly does not transfer to the real world, where there is little likelihood that a message will even be noticed, and where there is usually a significant lag in time between a message being seen and the desired behavioural effect.

Imagine you're sending a memo around the office reminding people not to steal other people's sandwiches from the communal fridge (yeah, *Gary*!). Firstly, that message may well remain unread and hidden in an inbox full of more pressing emails; and if it is opened at all, it may well be simply skimmed and forgotten. Secondly, the intended influence on behaviour is unlikely to be for another few hours, at best.

It is for this reason that research has shown that messages which are highly arousing (i.e. catch attention) are more likely to be successful, as are those which are more memorable. For example, an experiment by neuroscientists at UCL in conjunction with Ehrenberg-Bass Institute for Marketing Science and the brand Mars investigated which metrics were best at predicting the in-market sales performance of advertisements. Two of the top three most important metrics were hippocampus activation in the brain (i.e. memory) and parietal activation in the brain (i.e. attention).[37]

SO WHAT WORKS?

In summary, then, in contrast to standard models of communication, in order to be effective, messages need to take more of a non-conscious approach to their audience – using principles of psychology to get noticed and remembered, and 'nudging' behaviour rather than trying to change attitudes.

So what's the alternative?

A popular framework for understanding advertising effects is what's known colloquially as the 'path to purchase' – from awareness to purchase – as shown in the diagram below.[38]

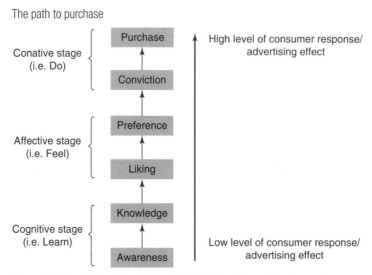

The path to purchase

Source: Adapted from Lavidge, R. J. and Steiner, G. A. (1961). 'A model for predictive measures of advertising effectiveness', Journal of Marketing, 25, 59–62.

While there is a lot of support for the first two steps and the final step (i.e. awareness, knowledge and purchase), which will be explored throughout this book, the other three steps are perhaps less robust. These three phases – liking, preference and conviction – form an attitude component and may actually play little to no part in the process of an effective message – since, as discussed before, the link between attitudes and behaviours is often weak or inconsistent, and since the majority of behaviour is driven by non-conscious factors. What matters isn't whether people consciously profess to like or agree with a message, but rather if that message is at the front of their minds when it counts.

So, this books suggests a three-step framework:

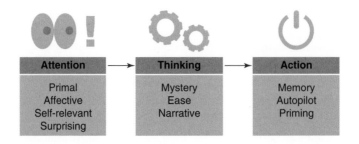

A Invite attention

As will be discussed, we have extremely limited attention spans, and there is a lot of information out there in the world; the first thing an effective message has to do is to get noticed. No matter what the goal of a message, if it doesn't even get noticed all efforts are moot. That email will never reduce staff absenteeism if it never gets read; that advert will never increase sales if people don't look up from their phones while it's on TV; and that pitch will never win the bid if the audience is chatting among themselves.

1 **Primal** Our attention is drawn to the primal – that is, faces, food and f-. . . sex. If we hadn't paid attention to these things throughout our evolutionary history, we would have had trouble spotting hungry tigers, finding scarce food, and propagating the species. Marks & Spencer's sexy 'food pornography' adverts increased food sales by 8.4%, for example.[39]

2 **Affective** We immediately pay attention to emotional things, like Mr Figglesnuff from before. Again, there are clear evolutionary reasons for paying attention to anything that looks like a baby, or anything which could be threatening, like a snake or a spider. Why not use both? To promote spawn-of-Satan flick *Devil's Due,* viral agency Thinkmodo filmed reactions to an unattended pram in New York – from which a demonic baby would pop up, screeching. The video garnered 50 million views, making it the eighth most popular video of the year.[40]

3 **Self-relevant** We automatically attend to anything self-relevant, or personal (like our name) – for obvious reasons. IKEA demonstrated this when they sent postcards to loyalty club members, giving a personalised weather forecast for the weekend following the postcard's arrival.[41] Compared to a non-personalised control group of recipients (i.e. a 'normal' campaign), the campaign increased sales by 7.5%.

4 **Surprising** We pay attention to anything which stands out from the patterns we're used to. We will, for example, always be fascinated with kooky pop stars and their meat dresses. When Heineken stood out from every other beer can on the shelf by turning theirs into a little keg, it resulted in a $300 million increase in revenue; to put that into context, the 'surprise premium' was such that the gross margin on the kegs was 17 to 20 percentage points greater than that on a typical six-pack.[42]

B Ignite thinking

Getting people to notice a message is the first step, but if they don't process the message, it will neither stick in their minds nor influence their thoughts and behaviours. Do students learn material better by reading a book, or by writing out the book in their own words and completing exercises? The efficient mental laundering of a message can be achieved with three techniques:

1 **Mystery** We are innately drawn to mysteries and puzzles because we want to close the gap in our understanding and resolve unpleasant feelings of tension. Jack the Ripper's last murder was 124 years ago; and there are still news stories speculating on his identity today.[43] Google posted a padlocked box to a group of 1,000 recipients, with instructions to search online for a specific phrase; when they did so, a Google Adwords advert appeared in the results, which led to the lock's combination and thus allowed recipients to open the box and read the materials inside; 95% followed the treasure hunt to open the box, and Google enjoyed a return on investment of 90 times its outlay.[44]

2 **Ease** Frankly, we are all very, very lazy. It's in our nature to save energy as much as possible, and it makes sense that it is so. For a message to be taken on board, it needs to be as short, simple and concrete as possible. Ingredients brand Knorr used the power of laziness in 2012 when they created recipe cards for meals using their products, as well as introducing meal solutions in-store by placing all of the items needed to make a particular recipe in the same location; compared to control stores, the power of simply making life easier and telling shoppers what to eat increased sales by 12% for their stock, for example.[45]

3 **Narrative** Social anthropologist Walter R. Fisher calls mankind *homo narrans,* or 'storytelling man'; indeed, storytelling is one of the oldest forms of human communication. It's how we make sense of the world.[46] In 2012, biscuity snack Twix produced an ad campaign which gave the brand a narrative.[47] Specifically, it created a backstory for the product, saying that the two bars were each made by different, rival factories – one made the 'left' bars and one made the 'right' bars. The campaign was a smash: UK sales volume grew by 37% and household penetration by 4.3%.

C Incite action

There is often a significant gap between the time a message is seen by an audience, and the time it's supposed to have its effect. What's more, psychological 'nudges' can be used to influence behaviour directly.

1 **Memory** Your message has to be remembered if it's going to impact behaviour in the future. To put it simply, we see a lot of stuff, and very little gets remembered. The Salvation Army conducted an appeal in

Canadian cities in Christmas 2010 which used the power of repetition to get itself remembered: specifically, their goal was that each person should see their messaging seven times.[48] This was achieved by communicating in the target cities via radio, newspaper, bus shelters and cinemas; donations increased by 32% and new donors by 8%.

2 **Autopilot** We have limited brainpower, which means that we can't think through every decision in laborious detail; instead, we usually rely on rules-of-thumb. Messages can utilise these to 'nudge' people into behaving a certain way. The NHS reduced the proportion of people who didn't turn up to prearranged appointments by 11% using a heuristic known as commitment: they simply asked patients to verbally repeat the time and date of their appointment to an NHS staff member.[49]

3 **Priming** Subliminal suggestion may be more fantasy than reality, but it *is* possible to influence behaviour by bringing certain ideas to the front of people's minds – for example, you can make people more self-centred and less cooperative by showing them some Monopoly money (it sounds just like Christmas).[50] Rye whisky Canadian Club increased its sales by 32% using priming: it used the phrase, 'Over Beer?' to make the idea of being bored of beer mentally salient.[51]

Before understanding exactly how these ten principles are achieved, we need to delve deeper into the brain.

THE MEME POOL

Let me tell you about Pepe the Frog.

Pepe is an anthropomorphic frog who has become a very popular mascot on image board forums – particularly the infamous 4chan.

Pepe has become so valued that rare Pepe images are, it seems, highly sought after. In March 2015, an eBay user set up an auction for over 1,200 rare Pepe images; bids reached into the high tens of thousands of dollars before eBay shut it down.[52]

What is it about Pepe that made him such a successful internet meme?

The word 'meme' was first coined by Richard Dawkins in his seminal 1989 book *The Selfish Gene*;[53] it means an idea or unit or thought, such as a word, an ideology, a fashion, and so on. Dawkins proposed that just as certain genetic traits excel in the gene pool through survival of the fittest, so do memes in the meme pool. Genes must survive and reproduce in order to succeed – the genetic trait intelligence, for example, enables survival (e.g. intelligent people are more likely to avoid dangerous situations, to exercise, and so on), and it aids reproduction (i.e. it is a sexually attractive trait since it is desirable to pass it on to one's offspring).

In the same way, memes must also survive and reproduce in order to succeed. That is, they have to be noticed and remembered, and shared. Successful memes have certain attributes which make this likely.

But what are these attributes? Memes like Pepe the Frog, Grumpy Cat, Gangnam Style, and others, going all the way back to the Hamster Dance, have certain things in common. They are weird, different and surprising. They are emotional. They are simple.

One experiment looked at what made YouTube videos go viral.[54] The most important feature was found to be *high arousal emotions* – that is, being exciting and attention-grabbing. Likewise, the aforementioned experiment on urban legends indicates that emotion, surprise, curiosity, narrative and simplicity all play a role in message success.[55]

We are starting to unravel the principles which help a message to get hooked in people's minds. Pepe is an example of a very successful internet meme – and all successful internet memes are examples of effective messaging.

EXERCISE

The meme pool

Think of five viral videos, pictures or news articles that come to your mind as very popular and/or memorable.

What themes do these pieces of viral have in common? Is there anything in terms of form or content that is similar across any of them?

SUMMARY

The science of communication

Do

✓ Take notice of how decision-making is influenced by social factors, and think about how that influences the effectiveness of communications.

▶

✓ Use the fact that people look to the crowd for guidance to understand the building blocks of getting messages hooked in people's minds.

✓ Harness the power of our innate desire to share things to make messages go viral.

✓ Realise that there is a huge difference between what people say and what they do, and recognise the massive implications of this for getting read and for understanding consumers more broadly.

✓ Aim to influence behaviours rather than attitudes.

Don't

✗ Take anything at face value, nor leave assumptions unchallenged.

✗ Treat people as entirely (or even mostly) rational: a huge chunk of the choices they make will be influenced by factors they are unaware of and which might not 'logically' make sense.

✗ Similarly approach effective messages as rational (the best messages go the 'peripheral' route and use emotional, sensory or implicit cues to influence behaviour).

✗ Speak to the mass rather than the individual; you need to speak directly to people if you want them to take action.

✗ Underappreciate the amount of 'noise' people are bombarded with every day! Think about how to cut through.

2 THE BRAIN

What stands out?

What are the first two messages you can think of from the last week? They can be any type of message – an email, a letter, a leaflet, an advert, a radio announcement, a poster, and so on. Write down the first two that come into your head. For each one, write down why that one came to your mind. What was special about it? What happened that was different from other messages?

Traditionally, theories of communication have largely been dominated by *homo economicus* – that is, the idea that people are rational actors who put careful thought into their actions in order to maximise the benefit to themselves. Of course, consumers *do* make rational choices. For example, in ultimatum games like the Prisoner's Dilemma, people generally make reasoned decisions that benefit both parties.[1]

However, to treat audiences as rational in this way is to only take into account half of the full picture (at most). Psychologists have long understood that there are essentially two systems in the brain: the irrational brain, and the rational brain. This distinction has been explored from as early as Freud's 'id' and 'superego',[2] to as recently as Kahneman's 'System 1' and 'System 2'.[3] In essence, the 'rational' brain is deliberative, conscious, slow and logical; the 'irrational' brain, meanwhile, is intuitive, non-conscious, automatic and emotional.

The System 1 brain can be thought of as Captain Kirk – intuitive, emotional and quick-witted – while System 2 is Mr Spock – rational, logical and deliberative. It's important to remember though that it's *Captain* Kirk and *Mr* Spock: one is very clearly in charge over the other, and this is just as true of the brain as it is of the *Starship Enterprise.*

System 1	System 2
(Evolutionarily) Older	(Evolutionarily) Newer
Tried and tested	New and buggy
Non-conscious	Conscious
Automatic	Deliberate
Emotional	Rational
Concrete	Abstract
Implicit	Explicit
Fast	Slow

Since – as we will see – Spock plays a far lesser role than Kirk, simply looking at a message's audience in terms of the rational brain is insufficient. To give an example, eye-tracking research has shown that 75% of prices are not even looked at *once* in-store;[4] similarly, one study found that consumers form lasting impressions of websites within just 50ms of exposure.[5] It seems, therefore, that conscious processes do not account for the entirety of attention and decision-making – much (if not most) occurs automatically and without conscious thought.

THREE BRAINS

So how influential is the conscious brain compared to the non-conscious brain in consumer behaviour?

The first thing to note is that the non-conscious mind typically takes precedence over the conscious mind. As Carter and Frith stated, 'Where thought conflicts with emotion, the latter is designed by the neural circuitry in our brains to win.'[6]

The reason for this is evolutionary. In the Triune Brain Theory,[7] it was suggested that the human brain is the result of the evolution of regions and their functions from one evolutionary ancestor to the next. Indeed, three distinct regions (i.e. reptilian, mammalian and human) are visible in the brain, as seen in the diagram below. Although this model is somewhat simplistic and outdated, the general principle has subsequently been confirmed by brain imaging research.[8]

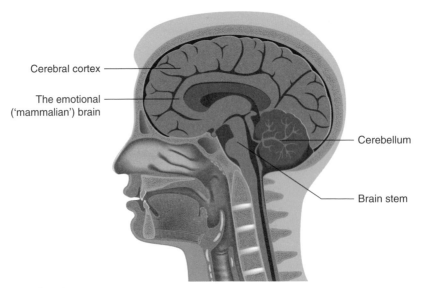

Cerebral cortex

The emotional ('mammalian') brain

Cerebellum

Brain stem

Source: © 123rf.com

The oldest and innermost part of the brain, known as the *reptilian* region, is comprised of the brain stem and cerebellum. This region is responsible for reflexes and maintaining homeostasis; it reacts to basic stimuli in our environment (such as a wasp flying at our face), and urges us towards base desires such as food and sex.

Next, around this part of the brain developed the *mammalian* region, comprising areas including the amygdala and the limbic system. This area is responsible for emotional, learning, reward and social processes.

Finally, the *human* brain – that is, the cerebral cortex – developed around the outside of the brain, and brought with it functions like planning, reasoning and language. The cerebral cortex is seen in the diagram above as the 'wrinkled' part of the brain. In fact, it is these wrinkles which give human beings their intelligence and the advanced cognitive functions which set us apart from most other animals;[9] the cerebral cortex being so wrinkled and folded means that it has a large ratio of surface area to volume – essentially, it means more brain can be squeezed into the same space.

The upshot of this model is that the emotional, automatic parts of the brain are evolutionarily older than the conscious cerebral cortex. Since the non-conscious brain has ensured our evolutionary fitness for longer, and since it is more deeply embedded in behavioural systems, it is more influential in decision-making. It is for this reason that, just as one cannot consciously stop oneself from sneezing or from flinching from sudden movement, the older brain regions and their goals will take precedence over the rational brain. Therefore, we cannot help but look at, say, pictures of a sexy topless model, despite, sometimes, our conscious preference not to.

COGNITIVE MISERS

The second thing to note is that the conscious mind is extremely limited in its capacity. Psychologists Shiv and Fedorikhin conducted a fantastic experiment in which participants were offered a snack of either fruit or cake.[10] Most people (59%) chose the fruit (which is somewhat surprising; I know what I would have chosen). However, when a second group was instructed to remember (i.e. keep in their minds) a seven-digit number, the majority (63%) chose the cake. Their conscious minds' capacities had been depleted by this relatively simple cognitive task, and the emotional, impulsive brain took over.

The important thing to bear in mind is that people are typically distracted, tired or busy when they receive any kind of message. Most people might be eating their lunch when they read Twitter, playing with their phones while watching TV, or working hard when receiving emails. Therefore it is the primal, cake-demanding monkey brain which reacts to messages most of the time.

Although it is impossible to quantify the subconscious, researchers have attempted to do so. Timothy Wilson looked at several perceptual experiments and was able to estimate that humans process around 11,000,000 'bits' of sensory information every second, but only 40 of these are processed consciously.[11]

So, the vast majority of attention and decision-making is non-conscious. Indeed, a great deal of research appears to support this theory. For instance, an eye-tracking study discovered that the speed of finding a brand was influenced twice as much by bottom-up factors (e.g. packaging, POS displays) as by top-down factors (e.g. planning to buy).[12]

The takeaway, therefore, is that the majority of decision-making is not conscious: rather, it is influenced by environmental cues, or *nudges,* and the primal, emotional brain. Therefore, when designing a message, it is vital to bear in mind that consumers rarely have the time or resources to carefully process it; instead, they tend to be affected by what gets their attention and what implicitly influences their behaviour, rather than rational arguments and information.

NEGLECTING THE GORILLA

Indeed, the suggestion that only 0.0004% of sensory processing is estimated to be conscious[11] has important implications for attention. To put it simply, we we don't have the resources to pay attention to every single message we come across; our attention is limited and we miss a lot.

You probably missed that the word 'we' was written twice in the previous sentence, for example.

A famous study by Simons and Chabris had participants viewing a video clip of two teams – one in white shirts and one in black shirts – playing basketball.[13] Participants were asked to watch the clip and count how many times the white team passed the ball to one another via bounces in addition to via direct throws; in essence, the task had participants focusing all of their limited attention on those dressed in white.

Half of them failed to notice a man dressed in a gorilla costume walk across the screen.

When participants in another study were asked to carefully observe a picture and extract all the important details from it, 42% of participants failed to notice a woman committing suicide off a building in the centre of the image.[14]

In 1953, Colin Cherry conducted a series of auditory experiments and identified a phenomenon he called the 'cocktail party effect'.[15] Imagine, if you will, that you are at a crowded cocktail party with your friends, and there's lots of noise around you: people are chatting, drinks are clinking, and Michael Bublé is playing on the stereo. You are engrossed in conversation with a friend, and everything else is simply white noise to you. Suddenly, however, you hear someone across the room say, 'I hate Bob, he's such a jerk.' (Your name is Bob.) Although you were not 'listening' to that conversation, and it was just part of the white noise in the background, you instantly become aware that this happened.

This example illustrates the way in which we only process the vast majority of information at a very low level; however, once something is deemed by the brain to be important, it focuses all our conscious resources on that stimulus.

To this end, there is believed to be a network of regions in the old brain that act as a kind of a nightclub 'doorman' or 'gatekeeper' who decides who can and can't 'come in'.[16] This part of the brain processes everything in the environment – all 11,000,000 'bits' of information – at a very low level, filtering out information that is deemed to be unimportant. This is why a third of brands receive no attention in store,[4] and why a great deal of information on websites is ignored.[17] Meanwhile, the brain's limited capacity to consciously attend to something – that allowance of 40 'bits' – is directed to that which the 'doorman' deems to be important.

So what does the 'doorman' have on his 'VIP list', which gets instant attention from the conscious brain? You are unlikely to get very far if you try to logically debate with a bouncer – in the same way, the brain's 'bouncer' prioritises the emotional over the rational.

In Richard Dawkins' *The Selfish Gene* he proposes that all animals, including humans, are nothing more than robots who exist simply to serve the goals of their genes – to survive and to reproduce.[18] Anything which helps achieve this goal (e.g. sex) is therefore important to the older, emotional brain regions, and will demand our attention.

LAZY BONES

Another implication of consumers having a limited cognitive capacity is that they tend to avoid a decision if it is too difficult. Energy (both physical and mental) is a finite resource, and it makes evolutionary sense that we should be hardwired to conserve it. This is why we have to 'pay' attention.

A famous study by Iyengar and Lepper set up a stall selling jams in a supermarket; the stall either sold 24 different flavours of jam, or just six. When there were 24 flavours, only 3% of browsers bought a jar; however, when the range was reduced to six, this figure rose to 30%.[19] When a decision is too difficult, people will often generally avoid it. Intriguingly, research has likewise shown that even qualified doctors are 19% more likely to prescribe medication if there is only one option available, rather than a choice of two.[20]

The upshot is that messages should place as little decision-making burden as possible on the shoulders of the audience: a message must be as easy as possible to notice and process, and it should make its desired action as simple as possible. Exactly how to do this will be explored in the rest of the book.

HOW MEMORY WORKS

The final brain science principle to address is the Spreading Activation Theory (ACT) of memory.[21] Once a message has gained a viewer's attention, it then needs to be processed – and this involves the viewer's existing memory structures. ACT proposes that memory is made up of a web of interconnecting nodes of varying strengths. For instance, the memory of a chair is connected to the memory of a table (which is, in turn, connected to a meal), and less so to a cushion and a pouf.

As will be discussed later in the book, with respect to this theory, messages encourage processing in three ways: firstly, audiences are motivated to process a message when the connection between two memory nodes is not immediately apparent (curiosity); secondly, audiences can process and remember a message more easily when it fits into existing memory structures and provides a meaningful connection between the parts (narrative); and thirdly, audiences can process a message more easily when the nodes are concrete, simple and frequently used (fluency).

Confused? This will be explained properly in Chapter 2.

THREE MONKEYS

Firstly, our conscious brains are so limited in their capacity for attention and decision-making, that 50% of the time they will completely miss a monkey walking across the room if they are engrossed in another task. Because of this, the vast majority of messages that get sent into the world will simply be ignored.

Secondly, we all have within our human brains a monkey brain, which, despite what we might like to think, is generally running the show. As a result, messages which appeal to the monkey brain using emotion and sex and so on are much more likely to be noticed; similarly, messages which let the monkey brain do the work, through being simple and utilising heuristic 'nudges', will be more influential.

Thirdly, those messages which adhere to these principles will be most successful. The Cadbury gorilla, for example, increased sales of Cadbury's chocolate by 8% in the UK, by being emotional and surprising – in essence, it was noticeable and memorable.[22]

SUMMARY

The brain

Do

- ✓ Be cognisant of the emotional and rational brains, and understand that everyone has a 'chimp brain' making lots of their decisions.
- ✓ Create messages that target both 'parts' of the brain – both human/rational (e.g. words), and mammalian/emotional (e.g. pictures).
- ✓ Make things as simple for recipients as possible.
- ✓ Design messages which take advantage of the 'VIP list' of the 'brain's doorman', so that people pay attention to them straight away.

Don't

- ✗ Expect reason to win out over emotion.
- ✗ Overload message recipients, since they only have a very limited amount of brainpower.
- ✗ Let your messages go unnoticed by time- and brainpower-limited audiences, who will just as soon miss a gorilla as a leaflet, email or presentation.

SECTION 1
INVITE ATTENTION

Source: © 123rf.com (spider, rock, rose); © Andrey Starostin (mushroom)

Which picture did you look at first? Chances are it was the spider.

There are certain stimuli which will automatically catch our attention. There are evolutionary reasons for this – if we didn't look at spiders straight away, we probably wouldn't have survived as a species.

Recall that our brain's 'doorman'[1] processes an estimated 11,000,000 'bits' of sensory information every second, but our conscious brain only has the capacity to attend to 40 of these,[2] so the 'doorman' directs this limited attention to that which is most important – like deadly spiders.

Now recall that there is a tonne of information in the world. Taking Facebook as just one example, over half of all users have more than 200 Facebook friends, and the average number of friends is 338.[3] That's a lot of status updates, photos and chats to process every day. Meanwhile, Ofcom reports that people spend an average of eight hours and 41 minutes a day on all media devices combined, and eight hours and 21 minutes a day asleep.[4]

These two points highlight why it's so important that any message gets noticed. Any message you send into the world is competing with two forces: firstly, there are many messages competing for attention; and secondly, that attention is *extremely* limited. Only a very select few messages make it.

A great deal of consumer research shows that simply being noticed is sufficient to influence behaviour significantly. For example, studies have shown that people are much more likely to buy a product if: it is placed in the centre of a shelf where it's easily noticeable;[5] a salesperson verbally suggests the product;[6] or an unusual point-of-sale display directs attention towards the product.[7]

A fantastic eye-tracking study illustrated this point by asking participants to make a series of choices between two brands in simulated shelf environments; however, sometimes one of the brands was made much lighter than the products surrounding it so that it was much more noticeable than the other brand. Before the study, participants ranked the brands in order of preference. The researchers discovered that, when people are rushed or distracted (as they typically are), how noticeable a brand is has a much stronger effect on choice than how much they like it.[8]

Similarly, when it comes to effective communications, you often only need to get your audience to notice or remember a message for it to have an effect on behaviour. Remember, for example, that anti-smoking PSAs can in fact increase the desire to smoke because they make the behaviour mentally salient;[9] interestingly, 'no smoking' signs can have the same effect.[10]

So, how can you make sure that your message is one of the select few to be noticed?

There are four types of stimulus that will get attended to automatically; audiences could not ignore them even if they wanted to.[11]

3 PRIMAL

EXERCISE

Uncontrollable urges

Can you think of a time in your own personal life when you were seemingly unable to resist your baser urges – and perhaps acted differently to how you might 'normally' act? How would you have acted differently in hindsight? And what was it that caused you to act this way originally?

I'm going to tell you a personal story – please try not to judge me. In my early twenties, I was in a 'hair metal' band (think Mötley Crüe). I was sure I was going to be famous – why *wouldn't* people go crazy for 80s glam rock in 2008? As such, and being a young psychology undergraduate, I spent my time trying to understand the psychology behind successful bands.

The first lesson I learned was that successful bands and musicians generally had to get people's attention. For example, one study of music videos found that physiological arousal was associated with positive emotions and preference towards that band.[1] Of course, being attention-grabbing is a clear goal of popular music artists – whether it's Elvis Presley wiggling his hips salaciously or covering himself in sequins, Miley Cyrus licking a hammer and rolling around naked on a wrecking ball, or Janet Jackson 'accidentally' whipping out her pierced nipple at the Superbowl (which went on to be named by Guinness World Records as the 'Most Searched-For News Item' and ostensibly helped her album, released the following month, go triple platinum[2]).

The second, related lesson was that certain themes in songs and music videos help to catch that attention – specifically, sex and violence. Or as some like to call it, 'sex, drugs and rock 'n' roll'. A content analysis of MTV music videos found key themes to include sex, violence and crime;[3] meanwhile, one review found that 28% of music videos contained violence, while 44% contained sexual content.[4] A review of the most popular songs in 2005 found that just over a third contained references to sex.[5]

The point of all this is that there are certain primal cues that have a high potential to grab people's attention. These cues are heavily related to the reptilian brain and its inherent urge to simply survive and reproduce.

While it's easy to dismiss the primal factors behind rock bands' success as little more than teenage hormones, there is plenty of other evidence which illustrates the reptilian brain's massive influence on society as a whole. Specifically, there is one lesser-discussed aspect of life that has seemingly been a driving force behind many of our greatest technological innovations: pornography.[6]

One of the earliest printed bestsellers, and thus a significant driving factor of the printing press' success, was *I Modi* (*The Ways*), a series of mythological engravings depicting a range of sexual acts – including sex aids and big penises.[7]

More recently, pornography was responsible for the success of VHS: the format was very expensive, but, people were willing to pay $100 or more for sex tapes they could watch from the comfort of their own home, and throughout the 1970s, 'X-rated' tapes accounted for half of all of Merrill Lynch's sales.[8] Since then, of course, pornography helped drive the popularity of the internet, with porn being believed to be the first product to make money online,[9] and popularising the practice of streaming videos.[10]

In essence, the primal has been a massive force behind the technological, and this state of affairs is nicely summarised by a quote from content aggregation website Reddit.[11] In January 2013, users of site were asked, 'If someone from the 1950s suddenly appeared today, what would be the most difficult thing to explain to them about life today?'

The top-rated answer was: 'I possess a device, in my pocket, that is capable of accessing the entirety of information known to man. I use it to look at pictures of cats and get in arguments with strangers.'

Indeed, excluding music videos, the most popular YouTube clip of all time is of a baby biting his toddler brother's finger and laughing.[12] Despite our haughty aspirations and technological marvels, most of our behaviour remains driven by the reptilian brain's primal urges.

There are three such types of stimuli which will draw attention to a message: sex, food and faces.

SEX

In 2014, a Russian media agency, AdvTruck.ru, had a fantastic idea for bringing attention to its new advertising spaces on the sides of trucks.[13] It used these spaces to advertise the service itself; the advert was of a naked pair of breasts accompanied by the company's name and telephone number, and the copy 'They attract'. There were 30 of these trucks driving around Moscow.

Within the first day, there were reported to be over 500 traffic accidents.

According to the *Metro* article, motorist Ildar Turiev explained, 'I was on my way to a business meeting when I saw this truck with a huge photo of breasts on its side go by. Then I was hit by the car behind who said he had been distracted by the truck.'

This is reminiscent of Eva Herzigova's famous 'Hello Boys' billboard for WonderBra, which was reportedly responsible for traffic accidents as well.[14] Both examples highlight the power of sex to completely captivate a person's attention and distract them from all other things.

In fact, beyond these anecdotal examples, a wide range of studies show that this is indeed the case. For example, an experiment by researchers at Indiana University demonstrated this with something called the 'dot probe task'.[15] In this task, participants are firstly asked to focus on an x in the middle of a computer screen for one second; this x is then followed for half a second by two images (one on the right of where the x was, and one on the left), and finally these two images are followed by a small dot where one of the images had been, on either the right or the left of the screen. Upon presentation of the dot, participants had to press a key on their keyboard to indicate whether the final dot had appeared on the left or whether it had appeared on the right of the screen. Participants could locate the dot more quickly when both of the images were neutral – in other words, when one of the images was pornographic, participants were distracted by it, and this interfered with their performance of the task. The pornographic images automatically and involuntarily captured the attention of participants.

Interestingly, this finding was found for both males and females. It might be tempting to dismiss the aforementioned examples as the results of simple-minded men who allegedly think about sex once every eight seconds (how was that statistic even found?), but the research suggests sex sells for women as well as men. The Diet Coke 11:30 'hunk' was a major success for the brand, for starters, with the 2015 gardener reboot enjoying social media sentiments that were 99% positive;[16] *Fifty Shades of Grey,* meanwhile, is one of the best-selling book series of all time.[21] At any rate, both men and women exhibit higher purchase intentions towards an advert if it contains an attractive model of the opposite sex.[17]

MEN ARE FROM MARS . . .

There are key differences between successful sex messages for men and women.

For example, one study used EEG (a measure of brain activity) to record levels of attention towards advertisements and found that, among men, attention to ads featuring women increased as the women went from clothed to semi-clothed to naked; however, among women, attention to ads was significantly increased by the presence of a man, whatever his state of dress.[18]

Other research has shown that sexual imagery in a print ad for a watch was only effective among women when the watch was framed as a gift being given from the male to the female; while the gift frame actually *worsened* the ad reaction among men.[19] Meanwhile, another study found that women had more positive reactions to a sexual advert when the ad was selling an expensive watch, rather than a cheap watch;[20] that is, sexual imagery was more effective among women when it was presented in the context of a rare, scarce and valuable product.

These findings are ostensibly explained by evolutionary differences in sexual desire between the genders.[21] It is generally believed that men are sexually attracted to good child-rearing properties like youth, wide hips and large breasts; women, meanwhile, are more attracted to resources that can provide for offspring, or traits that can be used to obtain resources, such as social status, strength, aggression and intelligence (inferred through creativity, wit, charm, humour, and so on). Furthermore, mating is much more risky and resource-intensive for women, meaning sexual attraction is more related to signals of commitment for women than it is for men.

To illustrate, one paper reviewed research, pornography and romance novels, and carried out a survey, to distinguish between male and female sexual fantasies. In line with the above, the researchers found that women's fantasies were less visual than men's and focused more on nonphysical characteristics; women's fantasies were more likely to unfold more slowly and involve more build-up over time; and, finally, women's fantasies were more personal and emotional and were more likely to focus on one partner, while men tended to fantasise about several.[22]

> This is ostensibly why the previous studies showed that nudity is more attention-grabbing for men, while symbols of plentiful resources, and the demonstration of male commitment through gift-giving, made sexual adverts more appealing for women.

Similarly, there is, of course, a strong evolutionary reason for why we pay attention to sexual stimuli. Remember that Dawkins suggests we exist solely to serve goals – to survive, and reproduce.[23] If we did not pay attention to sex as a species, we probably would not have done very well on the second front.

Pandas are a nice example. Pandas are currently categorised as an 'endangered species', with potentially fewer than 2,500 left in the wild, and a few hundred living in captivity in zoos.[24] The fate of the species ostensibly lies on these captive pandas' shoulders – yet, they simply don't want to breed, despite their handlers best efforts with Viagra, pornography and 'sexercise'.[25] As British conservationist Chris Packham suggested, perhaps it's time we just let them die out.[26]

Ultimately, sex is very good at getting attention, and thus helps to get messages hooked in people's minds. Incorporating sex into a message results in: more attention paid to it;[27] more thoughts about it;[28] more interest in it;[29] and better memory for it[30] – a smorgasbord of effects!

Let's take an example. During the 2013 Super Bowl, internet hosting provider GoDaddy.com aired an advert featuring an ungainly geek (apologies to the actor) *explicitly* making out with supermodel Bar Rafaeli. The advert was one of the best-remembered of the Super Bowl,[31] and had significant business effects for the company, increasing domain sales by 40% year on year the day after the ad aired.[32]

FOOD

Pinterest is an image-based site where users can manage and share their own projects, or discover other people's. Can you guess what topic is interacted with most on the site?

It's food – with one survey discovering that 57% of users interact with food content.[33]

If you use social media, you have probably not escaped the trend among users to take artistic shots of their food and share them. The trend is popular enough that the online restaurant reservation service OpenTable bought the Foodspotting app for $10 million in early 2013.[34] In fact, the trend is so big that French chef Alexandre Gauthier has had enough and banned food photography in his restaurant La Grenouillère.[35]

Part of the reason for the trend's popularity is ostensibly that food is very effective at grabbing attention.

For example, in one experiment participants were shown an array on a computer screen of either a food item, such as a strawberry, surrounded by visually similar non-food items, or a non-food item surrounded by food items (e.g. a red car surrounded by a strawberry and so on).[36] Participants had to find the location of the single food or non-food item surrounded by its distractors as quickly as possible. The researchers found that participants were significantly quicker to correctly locate a food item (surrounded by non-food) than they were a non-food item (surrounded by food). There is a strong attentional bias towards food.

Similarly, an eye-tracking experiment found that, when people are shown both a food and non-food image at the same time, their attention is much more likely to be directed towards the food.[37]

BE CAREFUL OF ATTENTION-GRABBING THINGS

There's an important point to be aware of in this part of the book. As discussed, it is, of course, vital to get people's attention or else a message won't stand a chance at all of being successful. However, it's important to use principles like food intelligently.

You do not want, for example, people to look at the tasty burger on your leaflet and completely ignore the name of the company and what it's selling.

We tend to pay attention to – and remember (as will be explored later on) – the most emotional thing at any one point; therefore, these principles, if not used smartly, may outdo the message they are meant to promote.

The key is to build the attention-grabbing stimulus into the message, rather than it be a disparate element. As will be discussed later in the book, faces are more effective in adverts when they look towards the ad's copy (i.e. grab attention and then direct that attention towards the message) rather than directly at the reader.

An important point to consider at this juncture is that it's not just images alone which bias people's attention; studies have shown, for example, that participants exhibit an attentional bias towards food-related words as well.[38] This point applies equally to the other principles discussed in this chapter: so emails, Tweets and letters are just as capable of using these techniques as presentations, adverts and displays!

Food is, of course, very important from an evolutionary perspective – if we, as a species, did not pay attention to food we would have died out a long time ago. One study estimated that just under one in ten thoughts are food-related.[39]

Evolutionarily speaking, an attentional bias towards food becomes even more important when considering that our ancestors used to exist in times of resource scarcity and uncertainty; all and any food that was noticed would have been eaten in order to stock up on fat and calories for when food may be less avaialable.[40] For this reason, high-calorie foods have been found to be more attention-grabbing than low-calorie foods.[41] Perhaps, therefore, it is no surprise that online food photographers are much more likely to share pictures of cakes, donuts or bacon than they are grapes, avocados or mushrooms.[42]

So, if you want to get your audience's attention using food, make sure you use a pizza or a hamburger – not a salad!

FACES

In 1994, Floridian Dian Duyser settled into her kitchen to eat a nice piece of cheese on toast she had just removed from the grill.[43] The 42-year-old took one bite from the dish before looking down and realising she could eat no more. She explained, 'When I took a bite out of it, I saw a face looking up at me – it was Virgin Mary staring back at me. I was in total shock.'

Duyser kept the sacred sandwich for ten years, during which it brought her, she claimed, a lot of luck – including $70,000 of winnings from a nearby casino. For reasons known only to herself, she decided, ten years later, to put the magical mouthful up for auction on eBay. There, the auction received over 100,000 hits, and the holy toast eventually sold for $28,000.[44]

Of course – whether Dian Duyser truly believed it or not – the Virgin Mary did not materialise in her toasted sandwich; rather, it was just a random pattern of melted cheese and burnt toast, and an example of the phenomenon known as 'pareidolia', where we see a face in what is actually a random pattern.[45]

Again, there is a strong evolutionary component to this: if we were unable to spot faces in the undergrowth from a distance, we, as a species, would regularly have been eaten by panthers.

In fact, the perception of faces is so vital to our survival that there is a specific area of the brain, the *fusiform face area,* which is specialised for just one function: the perception of faces.[46] Similarly, research has found that even newborns are predisposed to attend to faces; it found that nine out of ten newborns paid attention to a simple face-like structure (a light bulb shape containing two dots over one dot, like eyes and a mouth) but did not pay attention to the same shape flipped upside down. The researchers explained, 'There appears to be a mechanism, likely subcortical, predisposing newborns to look toward faces.'[47]

Experiments have shown that we exhibit a strong attentional bias for faces. For example, one study used the 'dot probe' task outlined above. It asked people to press one of two keys to indicate whether a dot was shown on the left- or right-hand side of the computer screen. Before the dot, however, two images were shown on the screen – one on the left, and one on the right. One of the images was of a face, and the other was of a non-face object. The researchers found that the dot was located significantly faster when it was on the same side of the screen as the preceding face image, suggesting that our attention is automatically drawn towards faces.[48]

When it comes to designing messages that get noticed, all this means that putting a face in a message will draw attention to it; as one paper put it, 'eyes always attract attention'.[49] In fact, if people are presented with a visual scene that contains a face, there is more than an 80% chance that they will look at the face within the first two eye fixations – that is, they will most likely look at a face before anything else.[50]

Taking online banner advertisements as an example, two researchers used eye-tracking and discovered that their participants spend around four times as long looking at adverts which featured a face than they did adverts with no face.[51]

So, if you want to get your message noticed, you could do worse than slap a face on it!

CEREAL MASCOTS

Have you ever noticed that children's cereal brands very often seem to have their mascot's faces on the front of the box? And that they're typically looking down from the box?

Source: © Richard Levine/Alamy Stock Photo

Researchers at Cornell University conducted two studies looking at faces on cereal boxes.[52] In the first study, they examined cereal boxes featuring 86 different mascots across ten different grocery stores in New York and Connecticut; they used the angle of the mascots' eyes to determine the height their gaze fell at four feet away (the centre of the aisle). It was discovered that the eyes of children's cereal brand mascots were looking at a spot, on average, 0.51m from the ground, while those of adult brand were looking at a spot 1.37m from the ground. The mascots are, ostensibly, making eye contact with their target customers.

In their second study, the researchers showed participants a box of Trix cereal, which either had the rabbit mascot looking at the cereal or making eye contact with the participant. Afterwards, participants were asked if they would rather choose Trix or Fruity Pebbles.

Without eye contact, 48% of the respondents chose Trix; but with it, this rose to 61%.

SUMMARY

Primal

Do

✓ Do absolutely everything in your power to stand out.

▶

✓ Engage the basest parts of audience's brains to make sure your messages get noticed.

✓ Use sex, innuendo and attractive people to get attention paid to your messages.

✓ Likewise use food – particularly high-calorie food – in messages to get them noticed.

✓ Use faces too.

✓ Use both words and images when applying these principles.

Don't

✗ Underestimate the simplicity of the factors that drive behaviour and decision-making.

✗ Shy away from the fact that sex sells.

✗ Neglect gender differences in what is sexually attractive – it can make or break a message's efficacy.

✗ Use highly attention-grabbing stimuli at the detriment of the actual message you want to convey – and bikini models, hamburgers, and so on, should not crowd out the message itself.

4 AFFECTIVE

Let me tell you another personal story. Again, please try not to judge me for it.

Throughout my life, up until a few months ago, I had *never* given money to charity. I had never donated a pound to PETA, a euro to the aged, nor a shekel to tsunami relief. The point is, I never gave my cash away to any cause.

One cause in particular to which I never donated was *The Big Issue*. As a Londoner, I encounter *Big Issue* sellers on almost a daily basis. Every single time, however, I essentially ignored the seller; I said, 'No thank you,' but every *Big Issue* seller failed to pass into that crucial 40 'bits' of consciously processed information, and I never bought a copy.

However, one day, I did pay attention. I noticed the seller and his magazine, and I bought a copy. In fact, I even gave the seller £10 and told him to keep the change, on a £2.50 magazine. (Watch out, Pride of Britain Awards.)

So, what happened?

Bob the Cat happened.[1]

Bob the Cat wouldn't let me use his likeness, so here's another cute cat instead.

Source: © Eric Isselee/Shutterstock.com

Thirty-six-year-old James Bowen had been a homeless heroin addict for over a decade; by 2007, he was on a methadone programme and living in assisted housing, selling *The Big Issue* to earn enough money to eat and keep warm. One day, James noticed a friendly ginger cat sitting near his home; after three days, it became clear that nobody owned the puss and James 'invited' him up to his flat, where James discovered he had an abscess in his leg. After James took the cat to the RSPCA, nursed him back to health and – importantly – named him Bob, the two were inseparable. Bob would hang around James as he busked, completely of his own volition, and he even followed James onto the bus.

James explains, 'Busking all of a sudden picked up, people were taking pictures, it went crazy. People interacted with me differently.'

Eventually, James would write a book about Bob, which would go on to sell over a million copies in the UK;[2] now, there may even be a Bob the Cat movie in the works.[3] In fact, in emails with the author *The Big Issue* disclosed that the magazine with Bob on the cover was one of their best-selling issues.

Bob is a fantastic example of the ability of emotion – or 'affect' – to have a massive influence on behaviour; as he said, his busking picked up and people acted completely differently towards him. This adorable little cat completely turned someone's life around through the power of cuteness alone.

And there's more proof – if it were ever needed – that we as a species go cuckoo for kitty cats. Cats were of course worshipped in ancient Egypt, it seems that they still are today. Google statistics showed, in 2013, that there were 368,000 searches a month on average for 'funny cats' and 673,000 for 'cat videos'; for 'cats', there were almost 40 million.[4] To put that in perspective, there were just over 11 million searches for Kim Kardashian. *Advertising Age* calculated that cat videos on YouTube generated over 1.6 billion views in 2012 alone.[5]

To consider some of the world's favourites, Nyan Cat was the fifth most viral video of 2011;[6] Lil Bub's YouTube channel has over 163,000 subscribers,[7] while Maru's has almost 500,000;[8] and Keyboard Cat was named the eleventh best viral video of all time by Huffington Post.[9] There is even the annual Internet Cat Video Film Festival, named the Cannes of Cats.[10] But perhaps the most outstanding example is Grumpy Cat,[11] who has not only featured on the covers on *The Wall Street Journal* and *New York* magazine, but also starred in the movie *Grumpy Cat's Worse Christmas Ever*; Grumpy Cat Ltd is valued at one million dollars.

PUG POWER IN ADVERTISING

While it's tempting to scoff at kittens and the rest as nothing more than intangible feel-good opportunities, there is a lot of evidence which demonstrates that, actually, cute animals (i.e. those exhibiting the *baby schema* – large eyes, a high forehead, and so on) or emotional animals can have significant concrete business effects.

The biscuit brand McVitie's introduced their *sweeet* advertising campaign in 2014. The adverts featured adorable kittens, puppies and other baby animals tumbling out of the biscuit packaging when it was opened. The campaign was credited with a sales increase of 3% and a market share increase of 26% across the total biscuit market.[12]

However, perhaps the most well-known example in the UK comes from the price comparison site Compare The Market, whose Russian meerkat Alexsandr Orlov and his 'simples' catchphrase took the country by storm. The advertising campaign resulted in brand awareness tripling from 20% to 59%, traffic to the website increasing by 400%, quotes increasing by 80%, and market share increasing by 76% while that of the brand's competitors fell by almost a third.[13]

The branding's so strong even a single, unrelated meerkat probably made you think of the site.

Source: © Simon_g

AFFECT: THE SCIENCE BIT

Let's go back to Mr Figglesnuff, the pug from the start of the book – do you remember him? Of course you do – that's the point!

Researchers at the University of Hiroshima carried out an amazing experiment looking at the effect of cute animals on attention.[14] Participants were asked to play a game similar to the family favourite 'Operation', where players use tweezers to remove small objects from holes without touching the holes' edges and setting off the buzzer. On average, all of the participants successfully retrieved just over half of the pieces without touching the sides – that is, just over seven, on average, out of 14.

After playing the game, participants viewed a number of images, which were either of adult animals or baby animals. Then, they played the Operation-style game again.

The second time around, people who were shown the adult animals spent the same amount of time on the game; they achieved a slightly higher score, successfully retrieving over eight of the fourteen pieces on average. This slight improvement was probably due to the fact that the first game had given them some practice.

The people who saw baby animals spent significantly longer on the game this time – about 12 seconds more on average. What's more, they also did significantly better, successfully retrieving ten of the 14 pieces.

The researchers proposed that the cute, baby animals share many of the same features of human babies, and that these features induce an innate caregiving response in humans; research has indeed shown that these baby-like features induce caregiving motivations and behaviours.[15] Baby schema cause people to be highly attentive in order that they can fully attend to a baby's well-being and be vigilant for potential danger.[16]

Similarly, it should come as no surprise that there is a strong attentional bias towards actual babies as well: for example, researchers at the University of Geneva found that people are quicker to correctly locate the dot in the 'dot probe' task (described previously) when the dot follows a baby's face, rather than an adult's one.[17]

This is at least partly why Evian's roller-skating babies advert was at one point name by Guinness World Records as the most viral video advertisement of all time.[18] The follow-up advert 'Baby&Me', featuring adults viewing their baby reflections in a mirror, broke records by garnering 20 million views in just two days and significantly increased the brand's market share in its key markets.[19]

Similarly, one of the most popular and well-known chocolate bars in Russia is Alenka; guess what it has on its packaging? A picture of a happy baby dressed as a babushka (a *baby-shka*?). In fact, researchers at the University of South Australia conducted an experiment looking at physiological responses to chocolate packaging with a happy baby on it.[20] Using facial electromyography, where electrodes can detect activity in the muscles associated with smiling and frowning, it was discovered that a chocolate bar with a happy baby on it was more emotionally arousing than one with no image at all.

In addition to a happy baby, the experiment also tried a barking dog. It, too, was more emotionally arousing than the blank packaging. From an evolutionary point of view, it is intuitive that we would instantly pay attention to threatening stimuli like a barking dog in order to survive.

In their paper 'Emotion drives attention: detecting the snake in the grass',[21] a team of three Swedish neuroscientists asked participants to, essentially, find a snake among the grass. Subjects were shown a grid with one randomly located fearful stimulus (a snake or a spider) surrounded by neutral stimuli (flowers or mushrooms) – or vice-versa (e.g. one mushroom surrounded by spiders). The data showed that participants were significantly faster at spotting fear-related objects surrounded by neutral ones than the other way round.

There is strong survival value in this – but sometimes it can backfire. Our extreme sensitivity to threat cues came to the fore on a Birmingham patio one spring day in 2012, when the RPSCA had been called out to a home to safely deal with a dangerous king cobra.[22]

It turned out to be a rubber toy.

Interestingly, the results also showed that the location of the stimulus in the grid did not have an effect on reaction times for snakes and spiders; however, neutral stimuli were located more quickly the closer they were located to the point at which the participant was initially looking. This suggests that the neutral stimuli were located using a laborious, deliberative process, while the fear stimuli were located in a pre-attentive, parallel processing stage; that is, the processing of emotional stimuli is automatic and non-conscious.

As an illustration of this point, one study used fMRI to measure regional brain activity in response to particular stimuli – in this case, neutral faces versus faces expressing fear. However, the stimuli were presented subliminally (i.e. for only 16.7ms) before being immediately 'masked' with a neutral image. This procedure meant that participants had no explicit, or conscious, awareness of the target faces – in other words, they couldn't 'see' them.[23]

Despite this, there was a significant brain response: areas of the reptilian and mammalian brain were activated in a region which the authors describe as an 'evolutionary adaptive neural "alarm" system'. A fantastic review of emotion perception by neuroscientists Marco Tamietto and Beatrice de Gelder suggests that visual inputs travel from the eyes at the front of the brain to emotional regions (such as the amygdala) located in the middle of the brain, before travelling to regions at the back of the brain associated with conscious visual perception.[24] All this means that emotional objects grab our attention before we can even begin to consciously appreciate what is going on!

VIOLENCE SELLS

Along the same lines as the prior studies, we are also hardwired to pay attention to violence – again, being very aware of any potentially impending danger is vital to the survival of all species.

In a test of the effect of violence on attention – and thus memory – researchers in Australia created four fake adverts for Coke Zero, which varied in how violent they were and how extreme the consequences were.[25] So, in a quarter of the adverts, a man is working on his computer with a Coke Zero, when a second man approaches him and puts a bin over his head (low violence) in order to steal his Coke Zero, at which point he says, 'Ouch' (mild consequences).

In another quarter of the adverts, the man instead has his head *stapled* and consequently falls to the ground screaming and clutching his head: this is the version with high violence and severe consequences.

Two weeks later, participants were asked to give the name of the brand in the advert. When the advert contained little violence – that is, a bin over the head – around a quarter of participants could recall the right brand, irrespective of whether the consequences were mild or severe. With the violent head-stapling advert, if the consequences was a simple, 'Ouch', 29% of participants recalled the brand; however, a staple to the head followed by screaming in agony on the floor meant the brand was recalled by a massive 56% of participants!

Meanwhile, a different study of violence in ads found that violence 'produced higher levels of excitement, attitude toward the story, attitude toward the ad, and attitude toward the advertised product'.[26]

WHICH EMOTIONS?

Moving on, including fear, which we've discussed, there are believed to be six basic, universal human emotions,[27] all of which capture attention (whether through faces, pictures, words, or whatever), and all of which have an evolutionary explanation.

Emotion	Detail
Fear	Research[34] with the 'dot probe' task showed an attentional bias towards fearful pictures like sharks and guns over neutral ones like furniture. Fear is adaptive as it helps us avoid harm.[35]

▶

Emotion	Detail
Disgust	Disgust is adaptive as it helps us avoid disease.[36] Research with the Stroop task, where people indicate the colour of a word, found slower response times for disgusting words like 'vomit', as they catch attention and distract from the task.[37]
Surprise	People are more likely to remember a fact if it is contrary to expectations.[38] Surprise is adaptive because it helps us understand, and so predict and control, our environment.[39] Surprise will be covered in full later in the chapter.
Anger	Anger is adaptive as it is protects against exploitation and helps to preserve equitable social relationships.[35] As discussed previously, people spot angry faces in the crowd quicker than other faces.[27]
Happiness	People can spot happy faces, presented very quickly, better than neutral ones.[40] Evolutionarily, happiness acts as a tracker and motivator of fitness and life success – e.g. being secure, having a partner, and so on.[35]
Sadness	Sadness is adaptive as it is the converse of happiness, letting us know if we are lacking something important, and motivating us to achieve it.[35] There does exist an attentional bias for sad stimuli, but it tends to be indicative of an affective disorder like depression.[41]

As well as these six basic emotions, there are other higher-order emotions, like love, jealousy and awe, which can be used for message stickiness as well. For example, researchers in France conducted an experiment in which a moneybox, soliciting money for African children in need, was placed next to a cash register in 14 bakeries. The moneybox contained one of three slogans across different stores and different days: in some cases there was no slogan; in others the slogan was 'DONATING = HELPING'; and in the others it was 'DONATING = LOVING'. On average, those who donated gave €0.54 in the control condition and €0.62 in the 'helping' condition. However, when the slogan contained the word 'loving', the average donation per giver was €1.04.[28]

The takeaway is that there are several emotions across a range of media which can be used to capture your audience's attention – for example, feature a picture of a shark in your PowerPoint when talking about your business' competitors, replace the word 'like' with 'love' in your Tweets, use emotional faces in your adverts instead of neutral ones; and so on.

However, there is ostensibly one important remaining question: which emotion should you use?

A study on *The New York Times* found that the only negative predictor of an article's popularity was sadness – a standard deviation increase reduced the likelihood of the article being shared by 16%.[29] Additionally, research suggests that sad faces and images *only* capture attention over other faces among people who are, for example, depressed.[41] Sadness, it seems, should be avoided – so are positive emotions more effective than negative ones?

While there is some evidence which shows, for example, that positive television messages are more likely to be remembered than negative ones,[30] there is a lot of other evidence supporting the power of negative emotions. For example, the aforementioned *New York Times* paper found that anger and anxiety were strong drivers of sharing, while another study found the same of disgust for urban legends.[31] Besides, one experiment found that, after viewing a list of 280 words in sequence, people were more likely to recognise negatively emotional words than neutral words: so even if positive stimuli are more effective than negative ones, the latter still have value over neutral ones.[32]

What's more, fear appears to be incredibly powerful – perhaps the most impactful emotion of all. A large review of almost 400 brain-scanning studies looked at the odds ratio of different emotional stimuli, compared to neutral stimuli, for activating the amygdala – which is essentially the brain's emotion centre.[33] Fear was the emotion most likely to have an effect, being almost seven times more likely than a neutral stimulus to activate the amygdala; it was followed by disgust (1:6.2) and sex (1:4.8). Fear is believed to be most basic and primal emotion.[34] As master-of-horror HP Lovecraft said, 'The oldest and strongest emotion of mankind is fear . . .'.

So what's the answer?

One of the two fundamental properties of emotion[35] is valence – that is, whether it's positive or negative – and, as we've seen, both types of emotion appear to catch attention. However, the other fundamental property is arousal – that is, whether the emotion is calm or exciting. This factor appears to be key in determining attention to an emotional stimulus; for example, words are more likely to be remembered the more arousing they are.[31] As a study of viral videos found, '. . . high arousal emotions are the primary driver of video sharing and while valance plays a role, it does so to a lesser extent'.[36]

How emotions vary by pleasure and arousal

	Low Pleasure	High Pleasure
High Arousal	Alarmed	Astonished
	Afraid	Excited
	Angry	Happy
	Tense	Aroused
	Frustrated	Delighted
	Annoyed	Glad
	Distressed	Pleased
Low Arousal	Miserable	Contented
	Sad	Satisfied
	Depressed	Serene
	Gloomy	At ease
	Bored	Calm
	Droopy	Relaxed
		Sleepy/Tired

Source: Data from Russell, J. A. (1980) A circumplex model of affect. *Journal of Personality and Social Psychology*, 39(6), 1161.

Importantly, one study demonstrated that, in order to be remembered, an emotional stimulus needs to be arousing (in which case it can be positive or negative), or, if not arousing, it needs to be positively valenced.[37] In other words, non-arousing, negative emotions (e.g. boredom, tiredness or sadness) should be avoided: they are quite literally depressing.

EMOTIONS AS MOTIVATORS

It is important to realise the powerful effect emotion can have, not just on drawing attention, but on motivating behaviour.

Fear, for example, can be incredibly effective at driving decisions. There is a fantastic sketch by the British comedy duo Mitchell and Webb in which a boardroom of toothbrush company executives are debating how to increase their profits – one suggests, to the others' early disbelief, that they might be able to convince people that they need to brush their tongues via raising awareness of 'microscopic antitongueanoids' and 'a gritty tongue surface'. Similarly, antiperspirant is believed to have become popular in the early twentieth century after advertising played on consumers' fears that they smelled bad. Messages can cleverly use fear – be it fear of death, loneliness, rejection, failure, or anything else – to drive their audience's behaviour in a certain direction. A meta-analytic review of almost 100 studies on fear appeals found that such messages – on topics like, yes, persuading people to brush their teeth – found that strong fear appeals are more effective at changing behaviour than low or moderate levels of fear.[38]

The Corsodyl campaign below, for example, used the power of fear to motivate people to use mouthwash if they suffered from bleeding gums – lest their

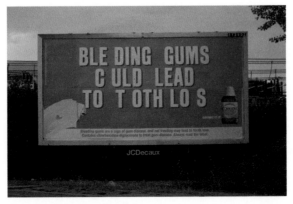

Source: © Jack Hinds/Alamy Stock Photo

teeth fall out. The campaign argued that you wouldn't ignore bleeding from your eyes, so why ignore it from your gums? Of course, the former is ostensibly much more dangerous, but the comparison was a smart use of fear as a motivator to buy. Corsodyl's initiative resulted in a 31% sales increase and a 2.3% market share increase in the UK.[39]

Whether it's drawing attention or motivating behaviour, the bottom line is that emotion works to make messages super sticky.

A study published in the *Journal of Consumer Psychology* had participants watch a series of clips of TV shows, in which some advertisements were sandwiched. Five of these adverts had been rated as neutral in a pre-test (an example being a voice-over discussing the merits of a new air freshener being shown on-screen), while five had been rated as emotional (such as an advert about domestic abuse featuring a Punch and Judy puppet show). Two months later, participants were phoned and asked to recall as many adverts as they could – they remembered two-thirds of the neutral ads, on average, but 95% of the emotional ones![40]

On a final note, marketing consultant Orlando Wood published a fantastic paper in 2012 which found that emotional adverts benefitted from tangible business results.[41] Low-scoring emotion ads achieved an average of 1.7 out of the four business effects, while the high-scorers achieved 2.7.

Emotion is such an effective principle for getting read that it is evident in concrete business metrics; more rational metrics like persuasion are poor predictors of message performance. As a study by Les Binet and Peter Field discovered, 'The more emotions dominate over rational messaging, the bigger the business effects. The most effective advertisements of all are those with little or no rational content.'[42]

SUMMARY

Affective

Do

✓ Recognise the amazing power of cute animals to stop us in our tracks.

✓ More broadly use baby schema – babies, puppies, kittens and so on – to instantly catch people's eyes.

✓ Keep an eye on internet trends (just like cat videos) to see what kind of things catch attention and therefore are useful in messages.

▶

✓ Use fear and violence to draw eyes on a biological level.

✓ Use emotion to motivate behaviour as well as catch attention.

Don't

✗ Be afraid of using things like cute animals out of fear of audience's perceptions – it's more important to be bought than liked.

✗ Feel that emotions have to be kept simple: higher-order emotions like love and jealousy are also effective.

✗ Use emotions that are physiologically depressing (like sadness); negative emotions are OK as long as they are excitatory.

5 SELF-RELEVANT

It was autumn 2014, and professional sword-swallower Roderick Russell was, despite the hardiness of his profession, starting to get a bit spooked.[1] After logging into Facebook, he would often notice that the adverts in the right-hand side appeared to know rather too much about him, as if his very daily movements were being monitored. For example, despite being a sword swallower, Russell had problems with vitamin pills: they made him gag. One of the Facebook banners, for vitamin pills, read, 'Does it seem ironic that swallowing swords is easy and then small pills make you gag?'

Russell started to go a bit cuckoo – he feared that his every digital move was being tracked, and he even stopped using his mobile for fear of being monitored.

It was at this point that Russell's roommate, Brian Swichkow, admitted he had been the victim of a cruel prank. Swichkow, a social marketer, had used Facebook's advertising platform to advertise directly to his roommate, by setting very specific demographic parameters for the ads.

The reason why Brian Swichkow's roommate noticed the Facebook ads so sensitively is because we are innately hardwired to attend to personal – or 'self-relevant' – information.

SELF-RELEVANCE: THE SCIENCE BIT

Earlier in the book we discussed the 'cocktail party effect' – where we can hear someone say our name even though we were not consciously listening to their conversation, nor most of the others in the crowded, noisy room.[2]

Since Colin Cherry's experiment over sixty years ago, a plethora of studies have supported the finding that we are hardwired to attend to personal stimuli. For example, it has been shown that: self-related information, more than other kinds of information, distracts attention and interferes with task abilities;[3] people are particularly good at detecting their name when it is flashed on a

screen, compared to other people's names;[4] and that self-relevant information is remembered much better than other information.[5] To illustrate the latter
point, people are more likely to recognise objects from a list if they were asked
to imagine owning the objects.[6]

French researchers published a series of experiments demonstrating the
extent to which we are hardwired to attend to personal information.[7] In the
first, participants sat in front of a screen and pressed one of four keys to indicate the location of the letter 'O' among three 'Q's in a 2×2 grid. However,
before seeing the grid, a stimulus was flashed for 250ms; this stimulus was
located in one of the four quadrants. When the stimulus was in the same location as the 'O', response times were faster, as one would expect, because
people's eyes had been drawn there. However, this effect was *enhanced* when
the stimulus was the participant's name, compared to someone else's name,
suggesting that our attention is even more drawn to the former. A second
experiment repeated this procedure, but this time the orienting stimuli were
presented below conscious awareness: an attentional bias towards one's own
name was still observed, even though the participants could not explicitly
'see' it.

Research in infants, meanwhile, has found that: infant babies instinctively
turn their heads towards noises that are familiar, such as the sound of their
parents' voices;[8] 11-month-old babies exhibit increased brain activity in
response to familiar words;[9] and children show an attention bias for their own
name as early as five months old.[10]

THE SHARE A COKE STORY

The principle has been used to great effect recently by Coca-Cola,
using what was perhaps one the simplest ideas in marketing history –
putting first names on their cans and bottles. Coca-Cola reports that
the initiative quickly evolved into one of the most successful marketing
campaigns in the company's history: there were almost a billion impressions on Twitter and 235,000 #ShareaCoke Tweets, and over 150 million
personalised bottles were sold.[11] The campaign has been credited with
reversing a ten-year sales decline in the US,[12] and increasing Coca-
Cola's sales in the UK by 4.93% when the cola market itself grew by
only 2.75% that year.[13]

▶

Source: © David Pearson/Alamy Stock Photo

THE NAME-LETTER EFFECT

There is a fascinating principle in social psychology called 'the name-letter effect', or 'implicit egoism', which appears to demonstrate that our names and initials have a significant impact on our life decisions – with, for example, Holly being more likely to prefer the brand Honda.[14] While the robustness of the effect has been called into question,[15] results have been replicated reliably,[16] and there appears to be an abundance of supporting research.

To elaborate, studies have variably found that: students whose names start with A or B get better grades in school than those starting with C or D;[17] there is a tendency for people to be social media friends with others who share their first name;[18] there is an effect on employer choice of one's own initial matching the company's initial;[19] the principle affects the stock market such that Susie is more likely to own shares in Starbucks[20] (and, interestingly, actor Arnie Hammer's grandfather was called Armand Hammer and he owns a great deal of stock in the company that produces – you've guessed it – Arm & Hammer!); one's name is linked to one's career, with Dennis and Denise being overrepresented among dentists;[21] people are more likely to marry a partner whose first or last name resembles their own;[22] and much more!

The name-letter effect can be used to help craft effective messages; let's take charitable appeals as an example. Researchers at the University of Michigan found that people are more likely to donate to relief for a hurricane if they share its first initial, as shown with the Hurricane Katrina example below.[23] Ultimately, personalising messages with people's names or initials is an effective route to getting read.

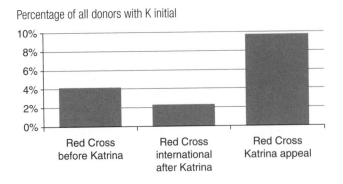

Percentage of all donors with K initial

PAYING ATTENTION TO OUR WORLD

Besides our names and initials, there are several other types of self-relevant stimuli which can be used as an attention-grab.

Other personal things we pay attention to include our own possessions. Researchers in Japan took photographs of umbrellas, shoes, bags and cups which belonged either to the individual participant being tested or to an unknown other (which were therefore unfamiliar).[24] There was found to be increased brain activity in certain regions in response to personally owned objects compared to unfamiliar ones, suggesting the former are more attention-grabbing.

Interestingly, another related technique is to use personally relevant language. Chinese psychologists conducted a test of brain activity while participants completed an object discrimination task – that is, pressing a key when a stimulus appeared. The researchers measured the effect of certain pronouns as stimuli: in particular, *ta de* (Chinese for 'his') and *wo de* ('my/mine'). It was found that, compared to the former, the latter produced a significantly larger P300 response (associated with attentional processes).[25]

Therefore, messages which make a personal appeal, use personal language like 'I am', and make their content personally relevant to their audience, are much more likely to hook their audience.

FAMILIARITY

We pay attention to things which are familiar to us, or 'on our minds'. Have you ever bought a new T-shirt or handbag, and then, walking through your daily life, noticed that many other people now seemed to own it too?

Perhaps the most well-known illustration of the aforementioned principle is the 'mere-exposure effect'. In his seminal study, Robert Zajonc exposed Western participants to a series of Chinese ideographs which, to the English-speaking participants, were essentially meaningless shapes.[26] Later, the participants were shown some of the same Chinese characters and asked to rate how familiar they were and how much they liked them. Exposure to the characters did not influence familiarity – that is, people didn't explicitly recognise them; however, it had a significant effect on preference. People liked the familiar shapes, even though they did not consciously remember them. Zajonc argued that this was due to perceptual fluency – that is, familiar stimuli are more easily processed, and this enhanced 'noticing' is mistaken by our conscious minds for preference. The most pertinent implication, though, is that familiar objects stand out.

Since Zajonc, many other experiments have demonstrated attentional priming (i.e. the direction of attention towards familiar, or mentally salient, stimuli). For example, one study found that priming participants to alcohol – by having them drink some of it! – resulted in an attentional bias towards alcohol-related stimuli.[27] People who'd had a drink of alcohol (compared to those given a placebo drink) performed worse on 'the Stroop task' of reading out the colour of a written word when the word involved was something like 'beer' – as their attention was drawn to the word, distracting them from the colour-naming task. The effect has even been found in pigeons: they'll recognise something more quickly if shown a picture of it beforehand.[28]

Putting this principle into practice, research shows that we pay attention to the faces of people we know[29] and love,[30] as well as familiar names.[31] A great case study comes from the pet insurance provider Affinity Petcare: they significantly exceeded their acquisition goals in an email campaign advertising their website simply by using each recipient's pet's name in the subject title.[32]

What's also useful, under this heading, is to utilise stimuli that are *personally familiar to everyone*. For example, there is evidence demonstrating an attentional bias to celebrities' faces;[33] celebrities have long been recognised as an effective route to message stickiness.[34]

Messages can also be made to grab people's attention through a consideration of what's likely to be on people's minds at the time the message is sent out. Researchers Jennifer Coane and David Bolata conducted a lexical decision task, in which participants had to press a button to indicate as quickly as possible whether the string of letters on screen was a word or not; testing occurred throughout the year.[35] The words on which participants were tested fell into various categories, including Christmas (e.g. *Nutcracker, Reindeer*), Easter (e.g. *Bunny, Lent*), Valentine's Day (e.g. *Cupid, Flowers*), and so on. There was a significant effect of congruency between time of the year and word type; in other words, people recognised words like *Leprechaun,* for example, significantly faster around St Patrick's Day. As a practical application of this point, one in-store survey found that, when asked to name a candy or soft drink, people were much more likely to mention orange brands like Sunkist or Reece's Pieces in the week preceding Halloween – because the orange decorations had brought these products to the front of people's minds.[36]

SEASONAL PERSONALISATION

Here are two great examples of brands using the principle of seasonal personalisation to increase the chance of hooking your audience:

– In 2007, Guinness produced an email campaign that was so good it won a Grand Prix at Cannes Lions.[37] On their birthday, recipients were emailed a video of a pub landlord wishing them a happy birthday and suggesting they celebrate with a Guinness and some friends. The email was opened by 60% of recipients, among whom 95% completely interacted with the video; each month, 30,000 people used the email to invite friends for a pint.

– Audi personalised an email campaign in 2012 by sending consumers emails around Christmas time featuring a Google Earth map showing the route Santa Claus would be taking from Lapland to the recipient's own home.[38] Audi reported that this email was the most effective out of all 250 emails the brand sent that year; the email was also the most cost-effective marketing action undertaken across the entire brand plan for that Audi model.

A FUTURE OF MASS CUSTOMISATION

Although stimuli personal to everyone are useful, technological advances fortunately mean that proper mass customisation is more feasible than ever.

A creepy example comes in the form of the American retailer Target.[39] The company made a sincere apology to an American consumer after his teenaged daughter received sales promotions in the mail for baby clothes and cribs; the father complained, 'Are you trying to encourage her to get pregnant?' (http://www.forbes.com/sites/kashmirhill/2012/02/16/how-target-figured-out-a-teen-girl-was-pregnant-before-her-father-did/).

A few days later, Target phoned the man to apologise again – but this time, he was a little sheepish. It turned out, his daughter was in fact pregnant.

Amazingly, Target's in-house statistical software had automatically analysed the girl's in-store purchases, and calculated that there was a significant chance she was pregnant. Certain vitamins and toiletries gave it away. So, with just some simple sales data, and an intelligent use of statistics, Target was able to predict the girl would have a baby – before her own father did so! And with the information, Target lived up to its name with a highly personalised communication which its recipient most certainly noticed and is unlikely to ever forget.

INNOVATIONS IN MASS CUSTOMISATION

Technological innovations are making it possible to produce dynamic hyper-personalised messages with an enormous attention-grabbing potential; we are, it seems, not too far off from a *Minority Report*-type future. Here are a few examples.

British supermarket giant Tesco has announced plans to introduce facial recognition technology in its petrol stations: the cameras will assess a customer's age and gender, and then play on-screen adverts targeted at that demographic.[40]

Meanwhile, *Marketing* magazine reported that Starbucks and L'Oréal both collaborated with O2 on location-based advertising: O2 users who opted into the scheme received a promotional message on their phone from Starbucks when they were near a branch of the franchise; likewise, those near a cosmetics store received a buy-one-get-one-free message from L'Oréal.[41]

However, perhaps the greatest tool available for mass customisation today is social media. By simply asking customers to plug into their Facebook account, companies can now extract an enormous amount of personal information – including personality, intelligence, happiness and more.

A fantastic paper illustrating this was published by the Psychometrics Centre at the University of Cambridge, who created a Facebook app for personality tests, allowing them to correlate Facebook data with individual differences.[42] Looking at 'liking' Facebook groups, they found, for example, the following links between traits and 'liking' Facebook groups: extroversion and Michael Jackson; introversion and anime; Indiana Jones and life satisfaction; The Colbert Report and intelligence; and the *Big Momma's House* movies and drug use (see Kosinski, M., Stillwell, D., and Graepel, T. (2013). Private traits and attributes are predictable from digital records of human behavior. Proceedings of the National Academy of Sciences, 110(15), 5802–5805).

This degree of personal information introduces a phenomenal potential for personalisation, and thus persuasion. Consider, for example, that personality traits are easily extracted from a person's Facebook profile (not to mention a wealth of other data points like their call logs); a paper published by Professor Jacob Hirsh showed just how useful this information is for producing messages that work.[43] Firstly, participants filled in the Big Five personality test. Then, they viewed five advertisements for mobile phones and rated them on six items like purchase intentions and brand interest, which were aggregated to form a measure of advert effectiveness.

Here's the key part: each of the five adverts featured copy that ostensibly appealed to each of the five personality types, such as 'Stay safe and secure with the XPhone' for neuroticism, and 'With XPhone, you'll always be where the excitement is' for extraversion.

Significant correlations between personality traits and ad effectiveness were only found when the two were congruent: in other words, the extroverted ad was more effective for extroverts, the neurotic ad was more effective for neurotics, and so on. This study is a fantastic illustration of how the 'big data' opportunities provided by advances in technology open up a huge degree of potential for persuasion.

Meanwhile, there is a lot of evidence illustrating how other personal information can be drawn from the internet and used to make messages more effective. In one study from UCL, participants went through a fake website for booking holidays, which featured web ads on some of the pages.[44] One advert, for an anti-ageing cream, featured either a photo of an anonymous older person or an age-enhanced photo of the participant him- or herself. Eye-tracking showed that people looked at the advert for almost twice as long, on average, when it contained a photo of their own face.

There is an additional plethora of studies looking at the effect of personalisation on email response rates. One experiment, for example, shown in the chart below, found that name data was a powerful route to effectiveness.[45]

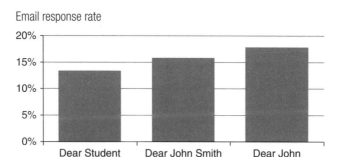

Email response rate

So, ultimately, in addition to the primal and the emotional, there is a third category of stimuli that will draw attention to messages and help them hook people – *and this time it's personal.*

EXERCISE

Future billboard

Imagine there are no limitations on technology and money. Your job is to create an interactive billboard to sit in the high street and communicate the message that people should pay their road tax on time. Think creatively and 5–10 years ahead, when there may well be an entirely free flow of data from a person's mobile device to devices around them. What functionality would you include in the billboard to make sure it grabbed people's attention? What would the billboard do and say in order to be as effective as possible?

SUMMARY

Self-relevant

Do

✓ Use personal information to catch attention – whether it's someone's name, their face, their hobbies, etc.

✓ Use personal pronouns to the same effect.

▶

✓ Keep abreast of the latest technologies as they offer amazing opportunities for message personalisation.

Don't

✗ Restrict yourself to only the things which are truly personal to individuals: there are also effective stimuli which are 'personal' to everyone, like seasonal decorations, celebrities, music, and so on.

✗ Forget people's concerns about privacy and security when it comes to personal data; they are also sometimes simply 'put off' by initiatives they see as creepy or intrusive.

6 SURPRISING

Source: © Guy Bell/Alamy Stock Photo

Damien Hirst's art will almost certainly have grabbed your attention just now because *it's surprising.*

There are two types of surprise to look at: one is basic and reptilian, like being surprised by a slap in the face; whereas the other is more cognitive, like being surprised by a bisected cow in formaldehyde in an art gallery. Let's take the slap in the face first.

CONTRAST

I always wondered why Michael Bay's *Transformers* films were so popular. *Transformers: Age of Extinction* was the first film of 2014 to make $1 billion[1] and its $90 million opening-weekend takings in China were an industry record.[2]

While global audiences love the films, critics loathe them: *Age of Extinction* has earned a measly 18% on Rotten Tomatoes. The films generally lack any plot, character development, narrative tension or intellectual interest; the franchise appears to be nothing more than just a bunch of big, noisy robots (sometimes grotesque racial stereotypes and sometimes featuring dangling robot testicles) smashing and clunking around and blowing stuff up. How can films that are nothing more than, as one Quickflix reviewer put it, 'an incoherent mess of noise and movement'[3] be so successful?

Well, actually, maybe that's the point.

The pop culture blogger Kyle Vanhove has done something very painful for the greater good: he has braved Michael Bay's filmography (up until *Transformers: Dark of the Moon*) and counted the number of explosions in each film.[4] This invaluable data, with a simple check of box office figures, gives us the chart below. The correlation is 0.94: the more explosions in the film, the more successful it is.

Explosions vs. box office for Michael Bay films

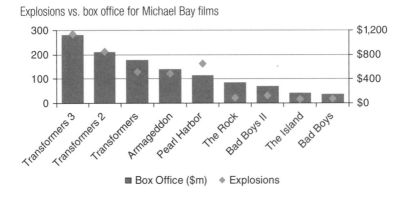

■ Box Office ($m)   ◆ Explosions

This (admittedly rather unscientific) example is a nice illustration of the first type of surprise – better known as 'contrast'. We are hardwired to immediately and uncontrollably pay attention to things that contrast with the environment in a very basic way, whether it's colour, movement or sound.

This phenomenon is known as 'the orienting response': the phrase was coined by Pavlov (he also called it the 'what is it?' reflex), and refers to the way in which we will react to sudden changes in movement or sound in our environment (like an explosion) by paying involuntary attention to the event before even consciously identifying what it is.[5] EEG research has shown that visual or audial contrast attracts attention involuntarily, and that it involves regions associated with attentional processes (the same as those discussed previously for personalisation and so on).[6] In fact, the orienting response has been shown to result in sensory receptors (e.g. eyes and ears) being directed towards the stimulus, a decrease in heart rate, increased skin temperature, increased skin conductance (i.e. sweat), and increased blood flow to the brain.[7]

Of course, such a response is, again, highly adaptive since it is useful in directing our limited resources to events that demand our attention, since they may be threatening, personally relevant, or otherwise beneficial to survival.[8]

Source: © USBFCO/Shutterstock.com

For example, you will probably have looked at this illusion because it appears to be moving.

Interestingly, on the point of Michael Bay's explosion fetish, there is evidence to suggest that the internet and television may be so addictive simply because they involve a lot of movement and visual contrast.[9] Several studies have shown that introducing lots of contrast into a television message (such as cuts and edits) results in increased attention towards that message.[10]

An experiment in the US selected a group of twenty one-minute-long television messages from adverts and TV shows; these messages were defined as being either slow, medium, fast or very fast in terms of edits (0–7, 8–15, 16–23 and 24+ edits, respectively), which were defined as a change in one camera shot to another within a visual scene. Arousal was measured using skin conductance and self-report, while a reaction-time memory test of visual recognition for the clips was taken after viewing. As can be seen, the more visual contrast or movement in a message, the more attention is paid towards it and the better it is encoded in memory.[11]

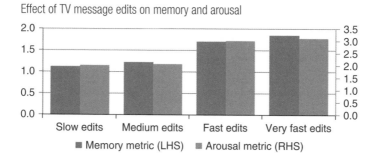

Effect of TV message edits on memory and arousal

Perhaps unsurprisingly, an article published in *Biologist* notes how drastically television has changed towards this trend in recent years: the article reports that a study of *Sesame Street* over 26 years found that the number of edits doubled during that time![9]

An important implication of this principle is that, whenever possible, it is better to use moving, rather than static, images and text.

Researchers from the University of Warwick and the University of Leicester sat participants at a computer to rate a series of 150 visual stimuli on distinctiveness using a six-point scale (lucky them!); a third of the stimuli consisted of static images, a third consisted of a 'film' of six static images arranged into sequence for 0.5s per image, and a third consisted of actual three-second videos. Then, after a day and, later, a week, the same participants viewed 150 visual stimuli – half of each type were new and half were in the original rating task – and pressed a button each time to indicate whether they recognised it from the task or not. As can be seen below, memory was significantly better for video.[12]

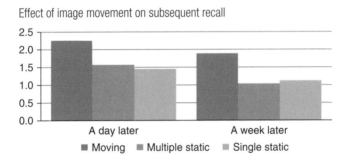

Effect of image movement on subsequent recall

As well as movement, attention is drawn to contrasts in colour[13] and light,[14] and, as well as visual changes, noise.[15]

So, imagine you need to create an ad for the radio, and there are certain key bits of information to which you want people to attend. What would you do?

Hopefully you have some good ideas by now (!), but a paper published in the *Journal of Advertising* found that noise contrast could be used to excellent effect.[16] Four radio advertisements were created with differing uses of background music: one had background music the whole way through; one had background music throughout but with silence underscoring the first vital bit of information; one was the same but for the third bit of information; and one had silence throughout. Participants heard one of the ads and, later, an unaided recall task asked them to write down everything they could remember about the ad they heard.

When silence underscored the entire ad, the average recall for a piece of information was 21%; when music was played throughout, this was 10%. However, when music was played throughout, except when silence cued the piece of information, recall for that information was a massive 65%. A clever use of contrast drew people's attention towards the information deemed key.

Meanwhile a fantastic series of in-store experiments illustrated how to use contrast in various ways to catch attention and enjoy tangible business effects – as shown in the chart below.[17]

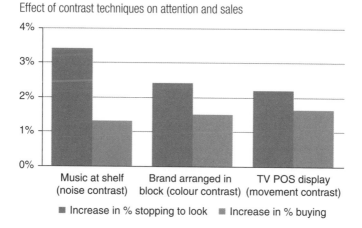

Effect of contrast techniques on attention and sales

■ Increase in % stopping to look   ■ Increase in % buying

USING CONTRAST IN-STORE

Contrast is an excellent way to improve promotional materials and draw shoppers' attention to a product. Guinness simply introduced cardboard fins which jutted out into the aisle and created contrast: the result was a 25% increase in sales during their use.[18]

As for communications more directly, a great example of contrast at play comes from online banner advertising. Animated compared to static ads increased recall from 24% to 48%, recognition from 56% to 76%, and click-through intentions from 3.3 to 4.1 (on a one to seven scale) in one paper.[19] And, while there's little doubt that we all absolutely despise them, banner ads with sound can increase recall from 9% to 15% and click-through rates from 1% to 7%.[20]

So, the takeaway is that messages can obtain stickiness through attention by simply using things which contrast with the environment – like noises, movement, or colours.

As a final example, Network Rail introduced to London's King's Cross train station a virtual assistant named Louise – a helpful, smiling woman who is projected as a moving and talking hologram onto a cardboard background to give verbal instructions to passengers to use the lift rather than the escalator if they have heavy luggage, which can clog up the escalator and pose a danger should it tumble down.[21] The manufacturer reports that Louise increased passenger numbers on the lifts by over 260%, and Network Rail has rolled the virtual assistants out in other stations across the country.

SURPRISE

Moving on, the second type of surprise is similar, but more cognitive and less banana in nature: this kind refers to the automatic attending to stimuli that are unexpected, distinctive or new. Whereas 'contrast' is about stimuli being different from the surround environment in some way, 'surprise' is more about being different from mental representations of the world.

For example, your brain probably went into overdrive when you read the word 'banana' just now, because the word didn't fit your predictions of how the sentence might have continued.

Researchers from the University of California published the results of a study which looked at this very thing.[22] Participants, wearing EEG caps to measure their brain activity, read a series of sentences of which some contained semantically incongruous words – like, for example, 'Other well-known reptiles are snakes, lizards, *eyeballs* and alligators,' or, 'Turtles are not as smart as mammals like *socks* or dogs.'

The data showed a large spike in brain activity when participants read the incongruous word in the sentence, suggesting these words resulted in a significant degree of involuntary attention and processing; as the researchers said, these words 'do not go unnoticed'. Their previous experiments also showed such words were well recognised and remembered, too.[23]

Essentially, the unexpected – or surprising – words resulted in attention. This was echoed in the results of the paper *An Experimental Analysis of Surprise*,[24] which presented participants with a pair of words on screen, one above the other. After the words, a dot appeared on screen for 100ms, either below the bottom word or above the top one, and participants pressed one of two buttons to indicate the dot's location. Participants did this 29 times; on the 30th trial, one of the words was written in white text on a black background, whereas all other words had been written in black on white. This broke with people's expectations; it did not match the pattern to which they had habituated.

When the dot was preceded by this surprising stimulus, people's reaction times locating the dot were significantly slowed, since their attentional processes had been diverted to the surprise.

In a similar vein to the unexpected, we also pay attention to the 'distinctive' – that is, stimuli which are unusual or different. For example, 'the distinctiveness effect' is a well-established phenomenon in psychology where memory is enhanced for stimuli that stand out from their surroundings as different: recall for the word 'diamond' in a series of sentences is enhanced for the phrase, 'The boy found a huge diamond in the applesauce,' over, 'The boy found a huge diamond in the jewellery store,' for example.[25] Similarly, another well-established finding is 'the isolation effect', which posits that a stimulus is more likely to be recalled if it is different from the other stimuli it is presented with: a digit placed in the middle of a list of nonsense words in one study was recalled in one experiment 71% of the time, while a digit placed in a list of other digits was recalled 48% of the time.[26] Likewise, 'the oddball effect' refers to the jump in brain activity, particular that associated with attentional processes, in response to a rarely repeated stimulus among frequently repeated stimuli in a series.[27]

A third and final type of this kind of surprise is 'novelty': we pay attention to stimuli which are unfamiliar or new in general, rather than just in a specific context. A robust psychological principle relevant to this context is 'the bizarreness effect', where attention and memory are much stronger for a bizarre, unfamiliar stimulus. A neuroimaging study found that brain signals were stronger in reaction to bizarre images (such as the head of a wrench grafted onto the body of a sheep).[28] This perhaps gives some indication as to what makes popular art successful!

Incidentally, the same effect has been found for verbal stimuli, too.[29]

THE POWER OF ORIGINALITY ONLINE

Californian artist – and one-time veterinarian – Sarah DeRemer has had her work featured in *The Guardian,* the *Daily Mail, The Telegraph* and beyond. What is it about her work that has been so successful and attention-grabbing? She grafts the head of one animal onto the body of another (in Photoshop!) to create what are now known online as 'hybrid animals'. The popular phenomenon has its own *subreddit* with over 30,000 subscribers and new images posted everyday – just one of which is shown below. As with all good ideas from the internet, it has since been ripped off by an advertising agency for Volkswagen.[30]

Source: 'Monkey Sparrow' by Sarah DeRemer.

One of the boards on 4chan is r9k, which utilises the ROBOT9000 bot created by popular webcomic *xkcd*: the attraction lies in the fact that the bot only ever allows new posts to be added to the forum. The bot's creator explained:[31]

 I was trying to decide what made a channel consistently enjoyable. A common factor in my favorite hangouts seemed to be a focus on original and unpredictable content on each line. It didn't necessarily need to be useful, just interesting . . . And then I had an idea – what if you were only allowed to say sentences that had never been said before, ever?

Surprise is, in fact, probably the most important predictor of virality online. A paper published in the *International Journal of Advertising* measured over 100 adverts on various metrics, and then noted the number of YouTube plays for each one: along with celebrities, distinctiveness was an important determinant of virality.[32] Similarly, the paper 'Why pass on viral messages?' asked participants to rate nine viral marketing campaigns in terms of the six basic emotions, including surprise, and found that surprise was the most dominant factor, being elicited by every one of the nine campaigns.[33]

An example of a viral campaign to successfully use surprise is the Mercedes-Benz 'Chicken' campaign, which was, simply, a video of a chicken whose head stayed in exactly the same spot while its body was being moved from left to right by a pair of hands.[34] The distinctive and

▶

unusual video clip had a huge effect on attention towards the brand: the clip exceeded the campaign's target by a factor of five by garnering five million views on YouTube within the first three weeks alone; of those who viewed the video, 8% shared it, making the video Mercedes-Benz's most successful online video ever; by the end of 2013, Mercedes-Benz was the most popular car brand on the internet, globally; the video had earned the brand 1.5 million new online fans.

Research by 'babyologists' has consistently demonstrated the power of the new to grab attention. Experiments have shown – as illustrated below[35] – that if an infant is shown a pattern they haven't seen before, even if it is as simple as a black-and-white checkerboard pattern, their attention will be drawn to it and they will spend a long time looking at it; however, over successive exposures to the same pattern, the number of times the infants look at it and the duration for which they look at it steadily decreases. Show them a new pattern, however, and their attention is piqued again! Another study, meanwhile, concluded that 'novel objects promoted exploratory interest at all ages'.[36]

Not only that, but developmental psychologists have given us key insights into *why* we pay attention to these kinds of surprising stimuli. Again, as with all traits (even, it is proposed, psychopathologies like autism[37]), there is an adaptive value to surprise – but what is it?

A recent study by two cognitive psychologists at John Hopkins University found that, when 11-month-old babies are shown something surprising that doesn't fit with their expectations, not only does it catch their attention, but the babies will focus on it and play with it until they have solved the mystery.[38] For example, babies shown a ball rolling down a ramp and then seeming to pass through a wall were then much more interested in the ball – banging it on the floor to test its solidity, for example – than those who seemingly saw the ball be stopped by the wall.

One of the researchers, Lisa Feigenson, explained, 'Our research suggests that infants use what they already know about the world to form predictions. When these predictions are shown to be wrong, infants use this as a special opportunity for learning . . . When babies are surprised, they learn much better, as though they are taking the occasion to try to figure something out about their world.'[39]

This is very evident in the facial expression characterising surprise, the 'surprise brow',[40] which comprises two features: firstly, the eyes widen and the

Source: © Ana Blazic Lavlovic

eyebrows lift, so that we can take in as much visual information as possible; and secondly, our jaw drops and our face and body becomes paralysed as our cognitive resources are diverted towards solving the puzzle at hand.

So, surprise is adaptive as it helps us to learn about the world such that we might be better equipped to understand, predict and control it; surprise is the driving force behind human knowledge and betterment.

Evolutionary psychologist Rainer Reisenzein summarised the literature on the topic: 'the feeling of surprise serves to inform the conscious self about the occurrence of a schema-discrepancy and to provide an initial motivational impetus for the analysis of the schema-discrepancy by eliciting curiosity about its nature and causes.'[41]

Surprise is, therefore, the first step towards interest, or *curiosity* – where surprise will catch an audience's attention, curiosity (discussed in the next chapter) is the following stage, where the audience cognitively processes the stimulus in order to figure out the riddle.

But, before we get to that, there is a huge amount of research exhibiting the practical value of surprise in crafting effective messages. Taking advertising as an illustration, many studies have shown that the more creative an advert is, the more likely it is to be paid attention to, deeply processed, recalled, or recognised.[42] For instance, echoing the distinctiveness effect outlined earlier, a brand slogan placed in the middle of a list of other slogans was better remembered when it stood out from the others.[43] Another experiment had participants watch TV shows with adverts sandwiched between clips; then, after a five-minute distractor task, they were asked to recall as many advertised brands as they could.[44] Control adverts' brands were recalled 28% of the time, while the brands in creative adverts (that is, those which had won awards for creativity) were recalled 41% of the time.

Importantly, a survey of advertising agencies in China discovered that campaign creativity was a strong, positive predictor of campaign success;[45] in fact, a series of interviews with American advertising executives concluded, 'Creativity is identified as the singularly most important factor in effectiveness . . .'[46]

A nice example is the 'Balls' advert for Sony Bravia, featuring 250,000 brightly coloured rubber balls bouncing down a street in San Francisco in slow motion;[47] Sony went from fourth position to the world-leading seller of LCD TVs in the wake of the ad, and increased its market share in Europe from 10% to 14%.

Ultimately, surprise is a very effective way to make a message stand out and be noticed – and it leads to deeper cognitive processing which is, as will be discussed next, the second key step to effective communication after attention.

CASE STUDY Jackpotjoy

In 2012, bingo website Jackpotjoy wanted to draw attention to its 'FUNdation', where people could submit their ideas for fun things to do and potentially have it come true out of the campaign's £250,000 bursary. The brand wanted to draw attention to the campaign in a fun manner. The solution: a huge rubber duck floating down the Thames.

Source: © Justin Kase Zninez/Alamy Stock Photo

The rubber duck was featured in 65 media publications and inspired over 20,000 hits to the 'FUNdation' website; what's more, the stunt increased unaided brand awareness for Jackpotjoy by 7% in the UK, and 10% in London.[48]

What's more creative than an enormous rubber duck?

EXERCISE

Create a web banner ad

Design a banner advert to be used on websites and advertise Dove's new facial cream, CreamEx2000. You need to make the banner advert surprising and unexpected in order to catch people's limited attention online. Don't just use movement and sound – be creative! In order to be surprising, first think of three typical conventions for web browsing or banner advertisements. What is the status quo for web pages or their banner adverts? Then, for each convention, write a way that your banner ad could break it in order to be surprising and unexpected. For example, one recent innovation has been to have the advert contain the entire screen until it has been closed by the user, breaking the convention of banner ads being at the top or side.

SUMMARY

Surprising

Do

✓ Use sudden movement and noises to get people to pay attention to your messages.

✓ Use movement over static images and text wherever possible.

✓ Skilfully use contrast to make messages, or parts of messages, as emphatic as possible (e.g. having loud noises except for the narration of the key message, when there is silence).

▶

✓ Use cognitive surprise as well (i.e. unexpected, novel or bizarre things).

✓ Be creative.

Don't

✗ Underestimate the power of simple principles like contrast in colour, light or movement to grab people's attention – the reptilian brain is very influential.

✗ Overdo it; again, you don't want the movement or noise to distract from or overcrowd the message itself.

✗ Annoy consumers too much as it can backfire in terms of message efficacy: people love to punish perceived unfairness.

SECTION 2
IGNITE THINKING

Getting attention is just the first step in hooking your audience; attention is necessary but not always sufficient.

Consider how many faces you see each day, how many times you hear your own name, or how many sexual images you see. Yet very few of these encounters will carry through into any sort of long-lasting effect on memory or behaviour, despite catching attention.

For example, one experiment tested the effect of faces on the success of banner adverts, and found that – just like our cereal boxes from before – faces drew more attention, causing people to look at the ad for around four times as long; however, as can be seen in the chart below, *recall* for the ad's message was significantly higher when the face was looking at it.[1] The model's gaze directed attention towards the words and encouraged their elaboration. So, while a face did draw attention to the ad, it was ultimately much more effective if it also enhanced the reading of the ad's copy.

Source: Adapted from Sajjacholapunt, P. and Ball, L. J. (2014). 'The influence of banner advertisements on attention and memory: human faces with averted gaze can enhance advertising effectiveness', *Frontiers in Psychology, 5, 166.*

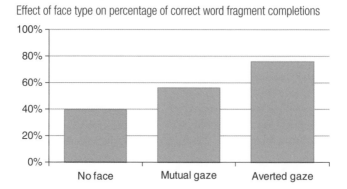

Effect of face type on percentage of correct word fragment completions

PART 2, SECTION 2 IGNITE THINKING

A series of interviews with senior advertising executives found that they believed in a clear two-step process when it came to effective communication: 'break through' and 'engage'.[2] Getting attention in a cluttered environment is part one; getting the audience to actually think about the message is part two.

Firstly, both attention *and* cognitive processing play an important role in memory;[3] depth of processing enhances memory for a message (and a message is more likely to influence subsequent behaviour if it is remembered, of course).

As an illustration, researchers at the University of Toronto showed participants 40 words and asked them to answer a yes or no question for each one.[4] There were five types of question, each increasing in the amount of cognitive processing required to answer it (indicated by increasing response times); after this task, participants were shown the 40 words, plus 40 new ones, and asked to indicate which ones they recognised from earlier. As shown in the table below, the greater the depth of processing, the more likely a word was to be remembered.

Depth of processing	Example question	Example answer		Average recognised later
		Yes	No	
Lowest	Is there a word present?	river	Fkxmhh	22%
2	Is the word in capital letters?	TABLE	table	16%
3	Does the word rhyme with weight?	crate	market	57%
4	Is the word a type of fish?	shark	heaven	78%
Highest	Would the word fit the sentence: 'He met a _____ in the street'?	friend	cloud	90%

As for the *why,* the 'Spreading Activation Theory' of memory[5] illustrates why depth of processing is so important; a crude illustration is given below.

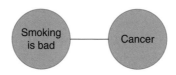

Low elaboration message: smoking is bad for you – it may cause cancer.

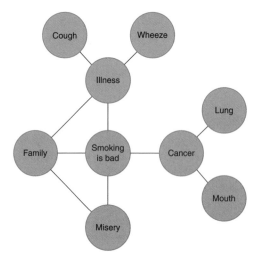

High elaboration message: think about how bad smoking is for you. Imagine the coughing and wheezing caused by lung cancer, mouth cancer – and what else? What do you think passive smoke is doing to your family – and how will they feel watching you die?

The elaborated-on message will be better remembered because the message has been linked to a greater number of memory 'nodes', and the connections are likelier to be stronger. Therefore the chance of the message being triggered in memory is increased: for example, thinking about family might trigger the memory of the elaborated message, but not the superficial one.

In addition, the elaborated-on message will be more persuasive because the audience has processed the message and what it means to a greater extent, therefore having a better understanding of it. For example, for the elaborated message, the audience will have a much better understanding of the potentially harmful effects of smoking, which will ostensibly better motivate their future behaviour.

So how do you facilitate the processing of a message?

7 MYSTERY

In autumn 2013, a YouTube channel called *Webdriver Torso* began to attract a lot of attention. Every single one of its unique videos was 11 seconds long, titled 'aqua', and comprised solely of red and blue moving triangles and a tone fluctuating in pitch. In the following months, the channel uploaded almost 80,000 of these videos.

Naturally, online enthusiasts gave their all trying to work out what it meant – as several media outlets, like the BBC, speculated, it may have been a secret code for spies, a viral marketing campaign, or even attempts to contact extra-terrestrials.[1] Until the mystery was revealed, the videos went completely viral.

Before we get into *why* this case generated such buzz, here's a brainteaser for you – see if you can work it out:

If I have three, I have three; if I have two, I have two; but if I have one, I have none. What are they?

Turn to page 237 for the answer.

Did you turn to page 237? How did it make you feel? Would you like to know the answer? Would you like to know, also, what the mysterious YouTube videos were for?

I bet you would!

We are all, as will be discussed, hardwired to solve mysteries and to close the gaps in our understanding. Whereas new, unusual or unpredictable things get our attention through surprise, curiosity subsequently causes us think about this surprising event in order to understand how it fits into our understanding of the world – and it can be a very strong motivator to process a message.

What, for example, would you do with a finished crossword at the back of a newspaper? Would you treasure it and keep it forever, going back over its factoids again and again?

No. You would throw it away.

A new crossword would sustain your interest since it contains puzzles to be solved – and gaps to be closed. In fact, there is a huge amount of research showing how puzzles like crosswords can be effective teaching tools since they pique interest in a curriculum's content by making it into an engaging riddle. For example, one paper reported that students given a crossword as a revision tool scored, on average, 76% on one sociology exam, while those simply given the key points to learn scored 69% – a significant difference.[2]

Similarly, another fascinating teaching tool is known as 'the mystery motivator'. In one study, five students were told that, if they handed in their homework on time and got at least 20 questions correct, and if they did so on an unknown and randomly assigned 'mystery' day, they would receive a closed envelope with a mystery prize in it: three out of five students showed an improvement in scores, with an average score increase among these students of 19%.[3] Another study found the mystery motivator technique to significantly increase compliance with bedtime requests.[4]

But, once the crossword is all finished, or the mystery envelope opened, an audience's interest quickly evaporates and they move on.

This might be why relationships so often fall apart once they become stale and predictable – there is nothing to hold the interest of one of the couple, and they get bored and discard their partner in favour of someone more interesting. Probably Chad the windsurfer with his sports car and talent management company (screw you, *Chad*). Interviews with 19 married women found that two of three key factors behind the passion waning in a marriage were the institutionalisation of the partnership and overfamiliarity;[5] and a series of experiments by a doctoral student found that boredom was a strong predictor of relationship dissatisfaction.[6]

THE CULTURAL POWER OF MYSTERY

The innate power of a mystery seems to be engraved into our collective consciousness. If it wasn't for Pandora opening that jar, we wouldn't have poverty, disease and death in the world (so it goes). Likewise, the power of curiosity was too much for Lot's wife and for Orpheus, both of whom couldn't help but turn around to have a quick peek, and ended up being turned into a pillar of salt and seeing his love being dragged back to Hades, respectively.

And recently, the secret and the mysterious have had enduring appeal in the stories we like to read and share. In 2014, there were, tragically, two air traffic disasters involving Malaysian Airlines. Both disasters were within 131 days of each other, both involved the same company, and both involved the total loss of life of everyone on board, over two hundred people in both cases. Yet, one

Relative google search data

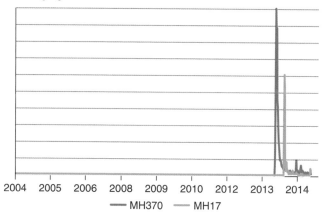

2004 2005 2006 2008 2009 2010 2012 2013 2014

━━ MH370   ━━ MH17

of the crashes received significantly more attention than the other; as can be seen in the Google Trends chart of searches above.[7]

Why? MH370 ostensibly received so much more attention because it was, and is, a *mystery.* There is no puzzle about MH17: we know it was shot down over Ukraine, and we've seen the wreckage in the news. But MH370 disappeared without a trace; what happened to the plane is a complete enigma.

Researchers at the University of Michigan published the results of a fantastic experiment in which participants were given thirty problems to solve, comprising maths, logic and spatial reasoning; afterwards, they were asked to recall as many of the problems as they could.[8] On average, participants recalled 33% of the problems they solved, but 45% of the unsolved problems.

It seems that mysteries stick in our heads.

A great example comes from the critically acclaimed television show *The Sopranos.* The final episode was aired in 2007, and yet there continues to be speculation in the media about the series.[9] At the end of the series finale, right before the expected denouement, the screen simply cut to black.

Many fans were outraged – they reportedly crashed HBO's website in their rush to complain[10] – and, even eight years later, speculation is rife about what the ending really meant, and what really happened to Tony Soprano.

Research suggests that shows like *The Sopranos, Breaking Bad, American Horror Story* and the rest, are, at least in part, so successful because of their use of curiosity through techniques like narrative tension and cliff-hangers.

For example, in one study, participants read one of two versions of a crime story, in which both suspects were equally likely to have committed the crime and so uncertainty was high, or where uncertainty was low since it was clear which of the two was the suspect; rated enjoyment of the story was significantly higher when the outcome was uncertain. More explicitly, the study found that ratings of curiosity were a strong predictor of enjoyment.[11] Similarly, a different study found that suspense is a very strong predictor of enjoyment when it comes to watching sports.[12]

In fact, I have another personal story to share on this topic. A few weeks before writing this, on a Saturday, I woke up late in the morning ready to work – I had an intense amount of work to get done (not least of all this book). Having got ready for the day and eaten lunch, I decided, 'Why not watch one episode of *The Sopranos*; what harm can it do?' I started watching at 1 pm. What time do you think I stopped?

6 am.

And it seems I'm not the only one. A survey of American adults found that 61% of them regularly binge-watch TV shows – that is, watch between two and six episodes in the same sitting;[13] and when Netflix released all 15 episodes of a new series of *Arrested Development* in 2013, it was reported that 10% of viewers watched all 15 episodes within a day.[14]

CURIOSITY: FROM SURPRISE TO INTEREST

So what is going on? Why do mysteries suck us in so much?

In his book, *Sweet Anticipation,* music psychologist David Huron proposes the ITPRA (Imagination, Tension, Prediction, Reaction and Appraisal) model of reactions to unexpected stimuli.[15]

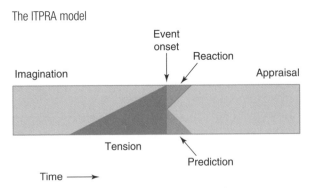

The ITPRA model

Source: Adapted from Huron, D.B. (2006). *Sweet Anticipation*, MIT Press.

Recall from the chapter on surprise that people show a significant increase in brain activity to incongruous words in sentences, like, 'Turtles are not as smart as mammals like *socks* or dogs.'

Let's take this as an example. In Huron's model, a person will initially listen to a song, hear a joke, or read a story; as they do so, they begin to imagine what the outcome will be, and they make a prediction. In our example, a person may be predicting 'mice' or 'hedgehogs' as they read, 'Turtles are not as smart as mammals like . . .'

There is a feeling of physiological arousal, or tension, as the reader reads onwards towards the outcome which may or may not match predictions. Depending on the outcome, and whether or not it matches predictions, the reader will have an immediate emotional or behavioural response. What's more, if the outcome doesn't match predictions, there is a period of appraisal, in which the brain invests resources in trying to understand the outcome and how it *does* fit with expectations – in our case, how a sock can possibly be a mammal.

It is at this point that the reader will move from surprise, the immediate response, to curiosity, the cognitive appraisal.

Noted psychologist George Loewenstein calls curiosity 'a form of cognitively induced deprivation that arises from the perception of a gap in knowledge or understanding'.[16] Indeed, curiosity is adaptive since it motivates knowledge-acquisition and exploratory behaviour;[17] it has long-since been identified as an appetitive drive similar to hunger or thirst.[18]

It is Loewenstein's 'Gap Theory' which explains this stage of cognitive appraisal.[16] When an outcome does not match a prediction, there is a gap between these two nodes in memory; we are motivated by the unpleasant feeling of cognitive dissonance to find the connection between these two seemingly unrelated nodes, as illustrated below.

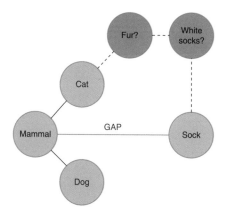

In a practical sense, there are ostensibly two uses for curiosity when it comes to crafting effective messages.

USING CURIOSITY TO MOTIVATE BEHAVIOUR

The first is to motivate behaviour – that is, to get an audience to actually read or interact with a message, or to otherwise influence some desired behaviour.

For example, one published paper tested the effect of different email subject lines on click-through rates and response rates for an email requesting participation in a survey.[19] The researchers found that both click-through rates and response rates were higher when the subject line did not include the reason for emailing; not only that, in fact, but both metrics were highest when the subject line was left entirely blank. Among the recipient list of high school seniors who had expressed an interest in the university, 17% clicked through when the subject line 'liberal arts university survey' was used; for a blank subject, however, 24% clicked through.

USING CURIOSITY IN MARKETING CAMPAIGNS

Secrecy and mystery also play an important role in marketing campaigns, generating significant interest in messages and products: from leaked copies of Harry Potter to speculating over the new Apple Watch.

A fantastic example of this comes from the marketing for the Batman movie *The Dark Knight*.[20]

Warner Bros created an alternate reality for audiences to explore, comprised of websites like IBelieveInHarveyDent.com where visitors could learn about the election campaign of fictional character Harvey Dent.

However, the viral campaign was so much more than this. At IBelieveInHarveyDentToo.com, a Joker-vandalised picture of Harvey Dent featured a submission form for people to enter their email address; for every person who did so, a single pixel was removed from the site's picture, ultimately revealing Heath Ledger as The Joker. Beyond this, the campaign led fans on a treasure hunt to learn new titbits of information, including searching through websites for clues, campaigning for Harvey Dent and giving out fliers, and rendezvousing at secret locations to be given mobile phones with recordings of The Joker.

In all, the campaign intelligently used the very innate urge to solve mysteries to generate significant interest in the film.

In terms of results, *The Dark Knight*'s website reached 1.5% of users on the entire internet, and, on the day of the film's launch alone, blog posts for the film accounted for 1.3% of all blog posts online. Of course, there were

▶

other factors at play, but *The Dark Knight* was ultimately a hugely success-ful film. It debuted on the largest number of cinema screens in American history, and took in $155 million in the US in its opening weekend.

USING CURIOSITY TO MOTIVATE MESSAGE PROCESSING

The second use of curiosity, however, is to encourage deeper cognitive pro-cessing for the message, in order to make it better remembered and more persuasive.

A key principle here is 'the generation effect' – that is, the finding that a message is significantly better remembered if the audience actually thinks it themselves, rather than just reading it superficially. Researchers at the University of Toronto assigned participants to one of two conditions: half of them read pairs of words that were associated in some way, such as rhyming or being semantically linked, like rapid-fast; while the other half were shown one word and the initial letter of its pair, like rapid-f___.[21] Afterwards, par-ticipants completed a test of recognition for the matched words. Those who simply read the words scored an average of 69%, while those who mentally generated the words scored 85%.

A wonderful application of the generation effect is illustrated by a study in which participants were shown one of two advertisements: one containing an instrumental version of the song *The Long and Winding Road*; and one con-taining the lyrics.[22] The participants were split into two groups according to their prior familiarity with the song. The next day, the respondents were asked to recall everything they could about the ad.

Hearing the vocal version of the song resulted in an average of just over one lyric being recalled from the advert, whether the participants were familiar with it or not. However, among high familiarity listeners, the instrumental version resulted in much higher recall – 2.1 lyrics on average. Because this group knew the lyrics, hearing the instrumental version caused them to generate the lyrics in their minds, resulting in much better subsequent recall.

This gives an interesting insight into McDonald's' 'Badadada-daaa, I'm lovin' it' jingle. At first, the adverts contained the whole jingle; now, however, the words are left off the end. The implication is that whenever a person hears the jingle, they mentally produce the lyrics themselves. The jingle causes a Pavlovian response of, essentially, thinking, 'I love McDonald's!'

The campaign, incidentally, had a fantastic effect on sales.[23]

The goal, then, is to use curiosity in the form of riddles or puzzles to get an audience to actually create the message in their own heads – what is known as 'co-creation'. But how do you make it happen?

PUZZLES IN MESSAGES

On the one hand, of course, it's possible to use very literal puzzles in a message. For instance, using questions instead of statements has been shown to increase message elaboration:[24] recall of information in a presentation was significantly enhanced by asking rhetorical questions rather than just presenting information. Similarly, simply asking people to imagine a message rather than read it has been shown to be effective.[25]

However, on a more subtle note, it is possible to engage curiosity and co-creation through the use of metaphors.

Metaphors work by presenting a small riddle to the audience. The definition of a metaphor is the application or juxtaposition of a word or phrase (the vehicle) to an object which is not actually applicable or related (the target). Since the two things are not literally related, the audience is presented with a puzzle to solve – that is, what is the connection between these two things? The result, as researchers have suggested, is the semantic and evaluative mapping of attributes from the vehicle to the target.[26]

Let's take a famous metaphor from *Romeo and Juliet*: 'Juliet is the sun'. Presumably, Romeo wasn't actually suggesting that Juliet is a massive sphere of hot plasma; thus, with this juxtaposition of unrelated elements, an audience's curiosity is piqued. How can Juliet be a sun? Loewenstein's gap theory tells us that the audience will seek to find the semantic connection between these two things and close the gap, and in so doing, the attributes of the sun are transferred to Juliet.

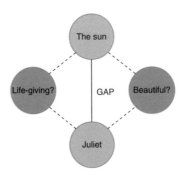

In this example, the audience subsequently ends up with an enhanced appreciation for Juliet's beauty. This is ostensibly why a meta-analytic review found the correlation between the use of metaphors and persuasion to be, overall, 0.07 – small but significant and positive – though this increased to 0.42 under optimal conditions.[27]

THE SIX TEMPLATES FOR PRODUCING CURIOSITY IN ADS

In their paper, 'The fundamental templates of quality ads', Israeli researchers analysed two hundred successful, high-quality adverts and found that the majority of them, 89%, could be categorised into six basic templates.[28] These templates are essentially metaphors: they present a small riddle which, when solved, transfers the attributes of one thing onto the advertised product. The six templates are:

1 **Pictorial analogy** A visual metaphor is used by presenting the product as something it's actually not, in order to transfer the qualities of that thing to the product. For example, a bottle of oil might be shown inside a corn husk in order to associate the idea of nature and freshness with the product.

2 **Extreme situation** In this metaphor, the product is shown in an extreme situation in order to imply the product has certain qualities. There are three kinds: the product has an extreme attribute; it has extreme worth; or there is an extreme alternative to using the product (e.g. moving to the North Pole instead of using a brand's secure locks).

3 **Consequences** These adverts use a metaphor to imply at the consequences of using, or not using, the product in order that certain qualities are transferred to the product. A famous example is the advert quoting, 'I never read the *Economist*,' by a 42-year-old management trainee.

4 **Competition** In these types of metaphorical adverts, the product is seen in competition with something else, and winning, so that the attributes the two things are competing for are transferred to the product. For example, an advert for a bread brand showed a child sleeping with her face on a slice of the bread, rather than a pillow, to communicate that the bread is soft and fluffy.

▶

5 **Dimensionality alteration** In these adverts, some dimension, such as time or space, is altered in order to highlight certain qualities of the product. A nicotine gum advert, for instance, showed a very old woman smoking in front of her birthday cake which put her age at just 42.

6 **Interactive experiment** These adverts are less metaphorical and more interactive, transferring qualities to products through game-based enhanced cognitive processing.

In summary, then, we are innately driven to explore anything that's surprising and arouses curiosity, which gives communicators the chance to pose puzzles and metaphors as a tool to encourage the cognitive processing of their message.

And, to put you out of your misery: the solution to the riddle is 'choices', and the videos were created by Google as an automated test of YouTube video quality. Hopefully(!), the frustration you felt at not knowing these answers until now gave you a taste of the power of curiosity.

EXERCISE

Keeping information secret

For each of the three sentences below, reword it so that it becomes an intriguing riddle or mystery. Below this reworded sentence, write the missing information which you have removed from the original sentence, and which people would find out by following or solving the mysterious message.

Six out of ten teenagers admit to staring at their smartphone under the covers at night.

Sources say Barack Obama and Hillary Clinton bicker regularly at the White House.

Please keep the communal lunch area tidy today for the health and safety inspectors.

Mystery

Do

✓ Make sure people process your messages at some cognitive level – otherwise it may be unmemorable and unpersuasive.

✓ Use riddles and puzzles in messages to get people to really think about what your message is saying.

✓ Use mystery to motivate behaviour (e.g. reading future messages).

✓ Use 'gaps' to easily create connections in recipients' memories.

Don't

✗ Be stale or predictable.

✗ Give everything to your recipients in one go or up front – they like to be teased!

✗ Feel that the 'puzzles' need to be overt: metaphors can also be very effective.

8 EASE

Take the chart below; what do you think it shows?

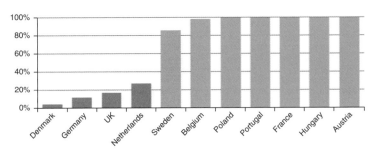

Source: Adapted from Johnson, E. J. and Goldstein, D. G. (2003). *Science*, 302, 8–1339.

This is data for consent rates for organ donation: the countries on the left are opt-in, and those on the right are opt-out.[1] Even with something as affecting as organ donation, people are generally happy to do whatever's easiest – in this case, sticking with things as they are rather than having to make an effortful decision for oneself.

This is a cognitive bias known as 'status quo bias': essentially, people tend to leave things as they are since change requires effort.

Recall that we are cognitive misers – we have very limited brainpower, not to mention physical energy and time, to spend on making choices and following up with them behaviourally. The upshot of this is that we tend to avoid decisions that are too difficult, and we generally take the path of least resistance.

People are so lazy, for example, that they will eat less food if it is simply placed out of their reach. Food psychologist Brian Wansink conducted an experiment with secretaries in an office, who were given an open bowl of Hershey's Chocolate Kisses to munch on.[2] The researchers counted how many chocolates the secretaries ate per day. However, there was a twist – the bowl was either placed on the secretary's desk, in her desk's drawer, or on a cabinet about six feet away.

The secretaries ate an average of nine, six and four chocolates per day, respectively. The harder the chocolates were to reach, the fewer the secretaries ate.

People are so lazy that they are more likely to buy a product if it's simply easier to see and reach. One experiment varied the shelf height at which a brand of crisps was sold in supermarkets in Reykjavic.[3] Positioning the crisps in the middle doubled the brand's market share: on the bottom and top shelves, the brand accounted for 4.0% and 3.3% of category sales respectively, but on the middle shelf the figure was 7.5%. Another study found that moving a brand from the least to the most accessible location in-store increased sales by a massive 60% on average.[4]

And *people are so lazy* that, given the free choice between walking up the stairs and taking the escalator in order to exit an underground train station, only 8% of people will take the stairs.[5] Interestingly, one study measured people's walking/running speeds from one point to another as they varied according to how much time was available – the data showed that people's instinctive strategies perfectly matched that calculated by a computer to minimise the amount of energy consumed.[6] We are hardwired to be as idle – or rather, as energy-efficient – as possible.

So – people are lazy! When it comes to crafting messages that will get hooked in people's minds, this fact of life has three implications.

SUGGESTION

The first implication is that people are highly susceptible to the power of suggestion. In other words, people will often simply do what they are told – to do otherwise might require effortful thought.

Going back to the study on people's choice of the escalator over stairs,[5] it was found that the proportion of people could be increased from 8% to 16% simply by introducing a sign saying, 'Stay Healthy, Save Time, Use the Stairs'.

One paper explained how a $5 intervention helped a small business owner increase her turnover to a phenomenal degree, using just the power of suggestion.[7] The $5 was spent on a cardboard prompting card for use by the business owner and her employees: the card served to remind the staff to ask customers, 'Would you like to buy a [dog chew bone toy] or anything else today?'

During a 12-month pre-experiment baseline period, when the customers were not prompted to buy anything, the shop sold an average of 6.4 pet products each month; during a four-month period when all customers were prompted with this suggestion, however, the shop sold a monthly average of 32.3 products. This small business owner's sales were transformed simply by, in essence, telling its customers what to do.

It could ostensibly be argued that the generalisability of this study, set in one small pet store, is questionable. However, a large-scale study of the South African credit market, involving over 50,000 recipients of a direct mail campaign advertising payday loans, found the principle to hold true.[8] In the study, a selection of recipients received a letter which featured a particular suggested use for the loan. This suggestion had an influence on loan usage; for example, among the customers who reported taking out a loan to pay off other debts, 3.6% more came from the pool of recipients receiving a letter suggesting just such a thing than from the pool of other recipients.

The power of suggestion is, of course, also highly prevalent online – e-commerce clicks are very much influenced by recommendations made to shoppers.[9]

Ultimately, messages can be made more effective by using suggestion to make it more likely that your audience absorbs the message you want them to absorb.

SIMPLICITY

The second upshot of our tendency to be lazy is that messages should be simple if they are to succeed; the truth is that audiences typically lack both the motivation and the resources to digest a long, complex message.

Remember – if something is too difficult, often people simply will not bother. For example, leading behavioural scientist Sheena Iyengar and colleagues looked at pension plans in the United States:[10] specifically, does adding more fund options – from, for example, a range of banks, insurers and investors – increase enrolment? In actual fact, no; Iyengar found that participation rates decreased as the number of funds offered increased, ostensibly since this made the pension plan more complicated. With all other factors being held equal, adding ten fund options resulted in a drop in participation rates between 1.5% and 2.0%; plans offering only two funds enjoyed a 75% participation rate, while those offering the maximum observed, 59, had a participation rate of 60%.

Simpler messages are – simply – more effective. As an illustration, the afore-mentioned South African payday loan study also tested the effect of letter simplicity on the take-up of loans.[8] Specifically, the letter presented the loan information in either a large, complicated table containing examples of different combinations of loan amount, duration and interest rates, or else a small, sim-ple table containing just one example of a loan amount, duration and interest rate.

The simpler table resulted in a 0.6% increase in the take-up of loans relative to the more complicated table; this was equivalent to reducing the interest rate by 2.3%.

Furthermore, not only does too much choice or information demotivate an audience, but the longer a message is, the less able an audience is to properly comprehend it, and therefore the less memorable and persuasive it will be.

In essence, people generally don't read the fine print. A study by the United States' Federal Reserve Board in Washington found that most borrowers do not know the finer points of the mortgages they have signed up to, and under-estimate or have no knowledge of the degree to which their interest rates could change.[11]

Returning to Timothy Wilson's estimate that only 40 out of 11,000,000 'bits' of sensory information are processed consciously,[12] it becomes clear that the more information is included in a message, the less likely it is that the key points will filter through.

A paper published in the *Journal of Advertising* describes how it selected two adverts for the same brand – one low in complexity and one high in complexity – by writing out the scripts for 88 television advertisements and submitting them to a computerised test of readability.[13] A sample of 81 stu-dents were asked to read a booklet containing scripts for five adverts; each participant's booklet was randomly assigned to contain either the low- or the high-complexity advert for the target brand. After a distractor task, the partici-pants were asked if they had read an advert for pasta sauce and, if so, which brand; then, they were asked to recall as many elements of the advert's script as they could.

When the advert was high in complexity, 75% of participants recalled the brand name, and they recalled 1.43 script elements on average; for the low-complexity script, however, 95% recalled the brand name, and the average number of script elements recalled was 2.59.

The simpler, the better.

As well as being short and simple, messages should make sure the most important information is easily noticeable: don't make it hard for your audience to comprehend your message. For example, when communicating online, the most vital pieces of information should go above the fold (that is, users shouldn't have to scroll down to see it) – a UX study of browsing behaviour found that users spend 80% of their time looking above the fold.[14] Similarly, whether online or offline, people tend to read from the top-left to bottom-right, and for this reason the most important information should be placed in the top-left, where attention is initially drawn.[15] Messages should make sure to avoid the so-called 'corner of death', the bottom-right.

CONCRETENESS

In a similar vein to simplicity, the third and final implication of the inherent laziness of our species is that messages should always be *concrete* over abstract.

Try, for example, to think of the word this definition is describing:

Noun. The rational investigation of the truths and principles of being, knowledge, or conduct.

Now try this one:

Noun. A piece of furniture upon which a person sleeps.

The first definition was for *philosophy,* and the second was for *bed.* The second word was probably much easier to name; this is ostensibly because *bed* is a concrete concept while *philosophy* is abstract. Concrete words have clearly defined, familiar meanings which are easily accessible, while abstract words are less inherently meaningful to us.

Concreteness enhances memorability and persuasion because it makes cognitive processing much easier: concrete concepts are retrieved and processed much more efficiently, while abstract concepts are more logical and less emotional, and are retrieved and processed slowly. Evidence suggests that abstract words involve linguistic processes in the brain, while concrete words more heavily involve nonverbal, semantic processes, although they activate linguistic processes as well.[16] To put it simply, concrete stimuli are more effective since they engage the 'monkey brain'.

Putting it all together, as illustrated in the crude diagram below, concrete messages will form quick and strong connections in memory, while abstract messages will form slow and weak connections.

Concrete message: 'Bob is smart'.

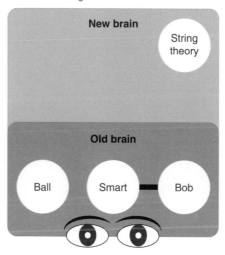

Abstract message: 'Bob likes string theory'.

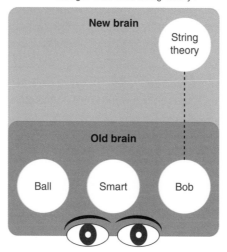

In support of this contention, an experiment by researchers in Massachusetts asked participants to press a button to indicate whether each sentence on screen – such as, 'The letter x appears in the word dexterity' – was true or false, while their reaction times were being recorded.[17] For each sentence, the target word, such as 'dexterity' in this example, was either concrete (e.g. 'bicycle') or abstract (e.g. 'honesty'). Reaction times were significantly quicker for concrete words than for abstract ones.

Similarly, another experiment read participants several lists of words, and subsequently asked them to recall as many as they could from each list.[18] On average, participants recalled 20% of the abstract words and 32% of the concrete words.

Putting this into practice, which of the two promotional display signs below do you think would be more effective?

MAKE A FISCAL TRANSACTION WITH THE UPMOST URGENCY!

BUY NOW!

A case study from nappy brand Pampers provides a real-world illustration. For many years, Pampers has collaborated with UNICEF to divert a proportion of profits from sales of the brand to children in need across the world; one of these campaigns comprised vaccinating babies against tetanus. In some markets, the packs featured the slogan, '1 pack will help eradicate newborn tetanus globally'. In other markets, however, a much more successful slogan was used: '1 Pack = 1 Vaccine'. This concrete copy has been credited by Pampers as being one of their highest return-on-investment programs; and the campaign provided vaccines that helped more than 100 million mothers and their babies worldwide.[19]

However, while concrete words are preferable to abstract words, images are more preferable still.

There is, for example, a great deal of research (stretching back more than a century[20]) demonstrating the existence of 'the picture superiority effect' – that is, that images are remembered significantly better than words. One study presented participants to 612 stimuli, of three different kinds, for six seconds each, and then conducted a test of recognition: participants recognised 88% of sentences and 90% of words, but they recognised 98% of images.[21] Similarly, research has shown that reactions when recognising images – measured either by brain activity or behavioural response times – are significantly faster than those when recognising words.[22]

Psychologists have suggested that this is because images are processed by non-conscious, automatic systems in the brain, while words are processed more consciously and deliberatively.[23]

To put it bluntly, while language may have developed as a human trait millions of years ago,[24] the ability to see has been with us since time immemorial; it is little wonder that images are more effective as communication tools.

Ultimately, the important point is that messages will be better comprehended and remembered if they use images. A meta-analytical review found that adding pictures to instructions resulted in a 40% increase in the recall of the verbal information.[25] On the other hand, other studies have found that people are quickest at solving problems when said problems are presented pictorially rather than verbally – and that mixing images with text doesn't lead to improvements over pictures alone.[26]

Perhaps, then, images should replace text in the most successful messages – at the very least, they should complement the text. However, one final, circular, point is that the more concrete – that is, simple and immediately meaningful – an image is, the more effective it is as a tool of communication.[27]

One final application of concreteness is tied up in the old adage, 'The death of one is a tragedy; the death of millions is just a statistic.'

Numbers, particularly large ones, are cognitively processed in an abstract, detached way and therefore have less influence over behaviour compared to more concrete concepts. Research has shown that emotional reactions are stronger when information is presented in a way that fosters concrete mental images, compared to a detached, abstract way.[28] For example, 'the identifiable victim effect' is where donations are significantly higher to appeals that highlight a single victim than those that focus on the large-scale problem at hand.[29] Similarly, purchases can be increased by reframing the price as a daily expense, like the number of cups of coffee per week the equivalent cost of a repeat donation would be.[30]

Therefore, it may be more effective to present a high number as, for example, the number of swimming pools it would fill!

Overall, messages can be made stickier by making the message as easy to process as possible, via the power of suggestion, via keeping things short and simple, and via using imagery and concrete words to get the point across.

EXERCISE

Putting ease into action

Turn the following statistic into something more concrete:
An estimated 10 million Brits suffer from depression.

Make this sentence more concrete:
Subsequent application of quantitative easing set to nullify recent confidence slump.

Simplify or shorten this sentence:
Brad Pitt and Angelina Jolie in supposed plans to move to outer Hampstead Heath.

SUMMARY

Ease

Do

✓ Whatever you want your recipients to do, simply use suggestion to encourage them to do it.

✓ Make messages as short and simple as possible – the longer a message is, the less likely it is to be read, and the smaller proportion of it that will be taken on board.

✓ Use concreteness (e.g. short words over long words, or images over words at all) to engage the emotional brain.

Don't

✗ Underestimate how lazy people can be!

9 NARRATIVE

One Saturday in April 2005, a rowdy group of spectators gathered at a coliseum in the Cambodian city of Kâmpóng Chhnãng to cheer on the bizarre fight unfolding before their eyes – the event was so hyped that tickets sold out three weeks beforehand. Despite the enjoyment of the crowd, the outcome was tragic. Within just 28 minutes, 12 midgets were dead and 14 were severely injured, including lost limbs and broken bones.

As it turned out, the assertion of the Cambodian Midget Fighting League's president, Yang Sihamoni, that his entire league of 42 midget fighters *could* in fact defeat a fully grown African lion, was incorrect.

An angry fan had taken umbrage with the league's claim that the midgets could 'take on anything: man, beast or machine', and brought his demand that the midgets fight a lion to Sihamoni, who arranged the fight and subsequently stated that, since the midgets outnumbered the beast 42 to 1, they would be able to 'out-wit and out-muscle' it. An African lion was flown in to Kâmpóng Chhnãng especially for the fight, which the Government allowed on the provisos that ticket sales be taxed at 50% and that no cameras be allowed into the coliseum.

What a story! As you might expect, it went viral and was picked up by publications like the *New York Post*.[1]

The only problem: it wasn't true. Two friends got into a heated discussion about whether or not a group of midgets could defeat a lion using the power of team work; one created a very realistic faux BBC News webpage, and the rest is history.[2]

This man-versus-beast tale is a fantastic example that – to paraphrase Mark Twain – often, we don't let the truth get in the way of a good story.

A lot of academic papers have been published illustrating the prevalence and power of narrative journalism. Academics have, for example, demonstrated how the US media played an important role in turning the senseless events of September 11 into a narrative of resilience, progress and heroism, allowing the nation to make sense of what happened and to follow a process of grieving.[3]

Experimentally, researchers at the University of Leipzig had a group of participants watch an episode of a television news programme containing nine clips for different news stories, one of which was about air pollution in Düsseldorf.[4] For the control group, this clip presented the information in a matter-of-fact way; in the experimental group, however, a clear narrative presented a protagonist who had been made ill by the air pollution, had a goal to reduce it, and was taking action to achieve that goal by protesting to the Office of Environmental Protection. Subsequent to watching the news, participants answered questions about what they had seen. Both comprehension and recall for the clip in question were significantly higher when it was presented as a story.

THE POWER OF STORIES

The fact is that information presented through narrative is much more affecting; it has the power to capture readers' imaginations, provoke fierce responses, and even ignite social change. Indeed, there are countless examples of stories rallying people and inspiring action, whether it's: a tired Rosa Parks refusing to give up her seat on the bus; Todd Beamer and his fellow passengers on Flight 93 who fought back against their hijackers; or the anonymous man who stood on his own against the tanks in Tiananmen Square. In her paper 'Contending stories: narratives as social movements', Professor of Sociology Francesca Polletta explains how stories provide groups with a unified identity and purpose and act as powerful motivators of collective action.[5]

It is little wonder that narratives are such a crucial social force: stories define us as a species – which social anthropologist Walter R. Fisher calls 'homo narrans', or 'storytelling man', since narrative is one of the oldest and most widely used forms of human communication.[6] From stories in Aboriginal cave paintings dating back tens of thousands of years,[7] to today, when spending on entertainment and media is worth 2.3% of global GDP – or $1.6 trillion[8] – stories are a major part of who we are. Simply put, we understand ourselves and the world around us in terms of stories: they allow us to give meaning to the world and to define our place in it.[9]

And, since they are so deeply engrained in our psyches, stories make very effective communicative tools; there is indeed a huge amount of research showing that stories make messages more memorable and more persuasive.

An amazing example of the power of stories comes from the *Changing Lives Through Literature* campaign in the US, in which convicts are given the chance to read, explore and discuss stories with one another, in the belief that stories can motivate life-long change.[10] Co-director of the programme, Robert Waxler, explained how the readers would come away with new outlooks and changed behaviours: one prisoner, for example, identified with the fisherman's struggle with the fish in Hemingway's *The Old Man and The Sea,* and this gave him the strength to resist the pull back into drug addiction.[11] A very recent study tested the effects of literature on 600 probationers compared to 600 control probationers who weren't part of the programme; the researchers counted the number of incidents for which the participants were arrested in the 18 months prior to, and following, the programme. For the control group, offending dropped by 26% over that time; but for those engaged with stories, offending dropped by 60%. What's more, the seriousness of the crimes was decreased relative to the control group as well.[12]

When it comes to crafting sticky messages, there is a lot of evidence for the power of 'narrative persuasion' – that is, presenting a message in a story format will make it more persuasive. For example, one study strikingly found that people could be persuaded to believe false statements like, 'Eating chocolate makes you lose weight', simply by inserting these sentences into a narrative;[13] similarly, another study discovered that people were more likely to become organ donors if they had watched a TV show in which organ donation was a featured storyline.[14] In his book *Tell to Win,* Peter Guber uses the metaphor of a Trojan horse: stories persuade because the audience readily accepts the gift of an entertaining story, and so unknowingly absorbs the message the narrator has craftily hidden within.[15]

In a large-scale experiment,[16] over a thousand students read 15 messages designed to persuade on topics ranging from the validity of aptitude testing to the use of cosmetics by women; for each message, participants rated how persuasive it was by indicating their agreement with statements like 'I agree with the writer's conclusion'. However, for each message, every participant was randomly allocated to one of four conditions, where the message: contained statistical information (e.g. '50% of crack users drop out of school'); contained narrative information (e.g. 'Joan was an A-grade student until she started using crack'); contained a combination of both statistics and narrative; or contained neither type of information. Ratings of persuasiveness varied significantly across the groups; as shown below, statistical information was more effective when presented in a narrative format.

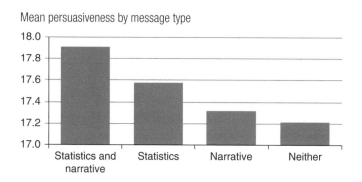

Mean persuasiveness by message type

Not only do stories enhance persuasion, but they also make messages more memorable.

The canonical form of a story consists of an introductory scene-setting, a beginning, a character acting to achieve a goal, and a final outcome – and research shows that people remember the outcome better when it is presented as the pinnacle of a story compared to when it is simply presented as information on its own.[17]

Participants in one paper read a story about an old farmer who owned a stubborn donkey.[18] In fact, some of them read the story, while others were presented with the same information, but not in a story format – it was simply a list of causally unconnected details. Having been asked to write down the passage verbatim as they could recall it, the people who read the plain information recalled 45% of the sentences, compared to a massive 84% for those who read the story.

So, stories work – but *why*?

Firstly, stories tend to be noticeable and memorable because they use many of the principles covered so far – like emotion, surprise and curiosity. Recall, for instance, that *Made to Stick* co-author Chip Heath discovered that disgusting urban legends were more likely to be shared;[19] and on the surprise and curiosity side, a great experiment measured the success of fairy tales by the Grimm brothers using the number of Google search results, finding that stories were more likely to be successful if they contained counterintuitive elements like talking mirrors or living gingerbread men.[20]

However, there's a lot more to it than that: there exist particular attributes of stories that encourage cognitive processing. Here are three reasons why stories make messages so sticky.

EMPATHY

When you hear a story, an amazing thing happens inside your brain.

To understand this, we first need to go back to the 1980s, when Italian neurophysiologist Giacomo Rizzolatti and his colleagues conducted a series of experiments which would go on to be extremely influential – although they didn't know it at the time. Rizzolatti *et al.* placed electrodes in the brains of macaque monkeys in order to record neuronal activity when the monkeys picked up pieces of food – but they discovered something amazing. The same neurons that fired when the monkeys picked up the food also fired when they simply *saw* a human researcher do the same thing.[21]

This was ultimately the first study of a great many in what was to be an exciting and seminal field – mirror neurons. Essentially, when we see someone else doing something, to some degree we experience it ourselves; when you see someone get slapped in the face, in your mind you get slapped in the face as well.[22]

Importantly, the same thing happens with stories. A meta-analysis of 86 brain-imaging studies found that the cognitive processes underlying social empathy are also activated by narrative:[23] when we read about a slap, we experience it ourselves. Interestingly, research has shown that people who read more books are more skilled at reading emotions in other people – that is, they are more empathetic.[24]

Researchers at the University of Washington had 28 participants read narratives about a young boy, Raymond, while they lay in an fMRI machine. Every clause in the story was categorised according to the presence or absence of dimensions like time (e.g. 'As soon as . . .'), space (e.g. '. . . returned to her desk') and objects (e.g. '. . . his English workbook'). Fascinatingly, reading a clause activated the brain region associated with that particular dimension. For example, reading about objects activated areas of the brain associated with hand movements; and reading about character's goals activated the prefrontal cortex, a region involved in ordering and structuring daily activities.[25]

Indeed, studies have shown that the persuasiveness of narrative messages is mediated by both transportability (i.e. imagining oneself in the story) and emotional processing.[26] In other words, stories are so effective because they are so affective; they make you feel and personally experience the message rather than just think it.

Pop culture comedy website Cracked has an interesting theory about this.[27] Many of the highest-grossing films of all time have something in common: they are animated, feature superheroes, or star wooden leading men. By using what is known in theatre as 'the neutral mask' – be it through the bland CGI felines in *Avatar,* the masked heroes in *The Avengers,* or the expressionless Keanu Reeves in *The Matrix* – films are allowing the audience to better imagine themselves in the protagonist's role. A simple, neutral face lets audiences transport themselves into the action – which, as research has shown, is vital for narrative to work.[28]

To sum up, the first reason stories are so effective is empathy – stories make your audience live and breathe the message, rather than just think it at an abstract level. When someone reads your PowerPoint bullet point, their rational brain will analyse the information – but with a story, they will personally experience it themselves.

FAMILIARITY

Take a group of very young goslings – if you move a cut-out in the shape of a hawk over their heads as if it were flying above, they will instinctively cheep, crouch and run for cover.[29] However, if the cut-out is the wrong shape, or if it is moved backwards rather than forwards, no such reaction is elicited from the chicks. This instinctive fight-or-flight reaction occurs despite the fact that the chicks have never seen a hawk themselves – and, in some cases, thanks to migration or continental shifts, their species has not seen a hawk for generations and generations.

The shape of a hawk, moving in the correct direction, is a key which unlocks a specific, hardwired reaction in the geese.

In the same way, we humans share hardwired – and learned – responses to specific stimuli. That is to say, we all, to some degree, share a common understanding of the world; we all use the same mental map. It is for this reason that stories make information easier to digest: they can hijack existing memory structures in order to transfer a commonly understood meaning onto a message.

Imagine, for example, that you wanted to communicate in a message that people should be wary of riding motorbikes because, even though they are beautiful, they can be deadly – and men should watch out that they don't get seduced into a dangerous situation. To communicate this message anew could be difficult and hard to comprehend; but if you were to use narrative to compare motorbikes to the legend of Medusa, the associations of the latter are instantly transferred to the former.

Consider, for example, the proposition that all stories throughout human history fall into one of seven basic plots.[30] These tales are part of our collective consciousness, and can be used to evoke shared understandings and transfer them onto a message.

Overcoming the monster	Rags to riches	The quest	Voyage and return
A protagonist sets out to overcome a monster or antagonist who threatens his way of life (e.g. *The Avengers*)	A poor protagonist acquires great wealth before losing it – he wins it back after having an epiphany (e.g. *Cinderella*)	A protagonist and his companions set out on an epic quest, with many trials on the way (e.g. *Finding Nemo*)	A protagonist goes on a voyage and returns a matured man (e.g. *The Hobbit*)
Comedy	Tragedy	Rebirth	
A humorous protagonist overcomes adversity to achieve a happy ending (e.g. *Mr Bean*)	A villainous protagonist falls from grace – their death or defeat is the happy ending (e.g. *Breaking Bad*)	A morally ambiguous protagonist redeems himself over the course of the narrative (e.g. *A Christmas Carol*)	

Similarly, in *The Hero and the Outlaw,* it is suggested that there are 12 archetypes in fiction, such as the caregiver, the jester and the lover.[31] Again, these shared understandings can be hijacked through narrative to make a message's meaning easily understood – in the case of *The Hero and the Outlaw,* the meanings can be transferred to a brand.

The innocent (e.g. Innocent)	The explorer (e.g. Land Rover)	The sage (e.g. *The Economist*)	The hero (e.g. Nike)
The outlaw (e.g. Smirnoff)	The magician (e.g. Apple)	The regular guy (e.g. Tesco)	The lover (e.g. Wall's Magnum)
The jester (e.g. Ben & Jerry's)	The caregiver (e.g. Heinz)	The creator (e.g. Lego)	The ruler (e.g. BMW)

In an illustration of this principle, a researcher at Vanderbilt University exposed participants to an advert in the form of either a vignette or a story, and then measured how closely the participants associated themselves with the brand with items like 'I can identify with Brand X'. The data showed that narrative adverts resulted in a significantly higher brand-self relationship, ostensibly because, as the author proposed, 'narrative processing may create a link between a brand and the self when consumers attempt to map incoming narrative information onto stories in memory'.[32]

To sum up, the second reason stories make messages so sticky is that they borrow from existing memory structures to make the message's meaning easily, instantly and universally understood. Stories implant a message's meaning into people's minds by hooking it onto memory networks which already sit there.

MEANING

In a landmark study published in 1944, a group of college students were shown a short film in which two triangles and a circle moved across the screen in an abstract fashion – and the students were asked to describe what they thought was happening.[33]

All but one of the students described the scene in terms of narrative – that is, social actors setting out to achieve a goal. One example included the explanation that the two triangles were men who were fighting over the woman circle, who, herself, was trying to escape.

The implication is that stories are how we make sense of the world; we interpret events in terms of cause and effect. This illustrates the third and final reason why stories make messages stickier – that is, they make information easier to comprehend by providing a semantic link between the parts.

The 'mnemonic link system' is a technique where a list of stimuli is made easier to remember by semantically associating each item with one another in the form of a story. For example, the list of words 'mouse, chair, sun, bus' might be better remembered by turning it into a narrative: 'The *mouse* sat in a *chair* under the midday *sun* and waited for the *bus*'.

Experimentally, participants asked to remember a list of six words in the correct order, could correctly recall 64% of the words when they were in the same category (e.g. apple, banana, grape), and 60% when they were not; similarly, they could recall 69% of the words when they were associated with one another (e.g. honey, sugar, sour), and 59% when not.[34] When disparate stimuli are meaningfully linked, they are easier to remember.

A fantastic example of this principle comes from *Chineasy,* a new system for learning Chinese from author ShaoLan Hsueh.[35] The system makes learning Chinese much easier by associating Chinese ideographs with pictures which convey what they mean – as shown below. The system gives semantic meaning to the unfamiliar characters, making them simpler to learn.

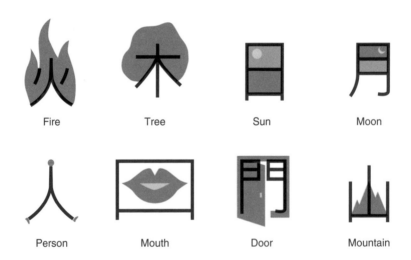

| Fire | Tree | Sun | Moon |

| Person | Mouth | Door | Mountain |

Similarly, research has shown that a set of stimuli is more easily remembered if they are causally related. In one experiment, participants viewed 32 pairs of sentences and then, subsequently, were given one of the sentences from each pair and asked to recall its match. The sentence pairs were of varying degrees of causal relatedness, as confirmed by a pre-study: for example, the lowest causal rating was given to 'Cathy had begun working on a new project' and 'She was carried unconscious to the hospital', whereas the highest rating was given to the pair which swapped the former sentence for 'Cathy felt very dizzy and fainted at her work'. Recall probability was about 10% higher for the most- versus the least-related sentences.[36]

Another study took this principle further by applying it to an actual narrative.[37] Participants read a story about pirates who were looking for treasure on an island; within the story, assertions about the natural world – such as 'Berry bushes are thickest on the windward side' – were inserted at either causal locations, where the alleged fact had an effect on what happened in the plot, or a non-causal location, where the alleged fact was mentioned but had no further part to play in the story.

Afterwards, the participants completed a test of cued recall – by, for example, completing the phrase, 'Berry bushes . . .' – and then rated each of the assertions on a seven-point scale of perceived truthfulness. As can be seen below, assertions with a causal effect on the story are both better remembered and better believed; the authors suggest this is because they are more deeply integrated into existing memory structures.

Effect of plot causality on message recall and believability

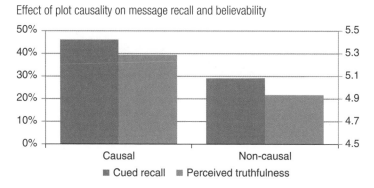

■ Cued recall   ■ Perceived truthfulness

To sum up, the final reason why stories are so effective is that they make messages meaningful: by providing a link between the different parts of a message, those parts become easier to process, comprehend and remember.

So, overall, narrative is effective because it makes an audience personally experience information, and because it makes processing easier by hijacking existing memory structures and providing a meaningful link between different elements.

And as for the power of narrative in a business context, this was fantastically demonstrated in a recent analysis of Super Bowl adverts.[38] The five-act model of narrative supposes that effective stories comprise five parts: the introductory exposition; a complication for the protagonist; a climax as the conflict develops; a reversal resulting from the climax; and a final denouement, or resolution.[39] Three expert judges rated the adverts shown during the 2010 and 2011 Super Bowls according to how many of the five acts they included; a measure of consumer reaction to the ads was taken from Spot-Bowl.com, where over 30,000 people rated the adverts on a one-to-five scale each year.

Ads without the full five-act structure received a mean rating of 2.4, while those with the five acts received a 3.4 average score.

Adweek reported that the most effective advert of Q1 2014 was indeed a Super Bowl advert – specifically, Budweiser's 'Puppy Love'.[40] The ad featured the heart-warming story of a Labrador puppy who makes friends with the horses on his home farm; when a man comes to adopt the pup, the horses menacingly block his way, and the story closes on both the horses and puppy triumphantly marching back to the farm to be welcomed back with hugs and kisses by the owners.

It may sound saccharine – but remember, *it worked.* Ultimately, infusing narrative into your message will make it very effective.

EXERCISE

Storytelling

You want to tell a story to engage and persuade audiences around cycling more and driving less. Create a story by coming up with each of the prerequisite parts, and then putting them together in a final narrative:

1 Setting

2 Character

3 Character's goal

4 Character sets out to achieve the goal

5 Conflict and tension

6 Climax of story and resolution of tension

7 Epilogue

Put it all together . . .

Narrative

Do

✓ Recognise that humans have been using stories to understand and share information since time immemorial.

✓ Use stories as 'Trojan horses' in which to feed information to audiences.

✓ Utilise narrative to easily form connections in memory and to easily communicate the intended meaning of a message.

✓ Make use of existing plots and archetypes to make understanding the message very intuitive.

Don't

✗ Focus on the importance of the story at the expense of the truth, however.

✗ Forget every element that is needed for narrative – that is, with a beginning, a character, a goal, an effort to achieve the goal, dramatic tension, and a resolution.

SECTION 3
INCITE ACTION

So far, we have addressed how to use attention to get people to notice a message, and how to use cognitive processing to get them to absorb it. But what should that message actually *be*?

Importantly, the way in which a message is put together can have a powerful effect on its ability to influence its audience.

To give an example, in the 1960s, the heartburn and indigestion relief tablet Alka Seltzer managed to use an extremely intelligent message to increase its sales significantly – not quite double their sales, but almost.[1] How? The brand introduced the slogan 'Plop, Plop, Fizz, Fizz', while plastering their packaging and advertising with imagery of *two* tablets fizzing in water. The subtle suggestion that two tablets were needed (when in reality one would suffice) had a massive impact on their sales (see http://www.snopes.com/business/genius/alka-seltzer.asp).

There are ostensibly two ways to influence behaviour via messages: one is through heuristics, or 'nudges', as demonstrated in the above example; and the other is through priming, which is, in essence, planting ideas in people's heads.

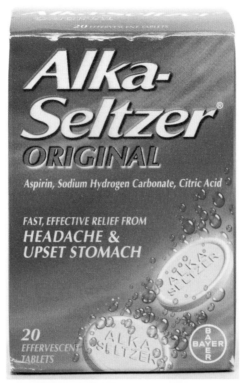

Source: © razorpix/Alamy Stock Photo

Before we get to that, though, it's important to remember that there is usually a significant lag between the time a person receives a message, and the time that message needs to have its effect. Say, for instance, you see a Tweet from Cancer Research UK encouraging you not to drink the next time you go out with your friends, which won't be until the next weekend; you may well have forgotten it by then.

In fact, advertising research has identified something known as 'advertising adstock', the memory 'half-life' of an advertisement – that is, the time it takes for awareness or memory of an advert to decrease by half.[2] Although this varies between adverts, it's typically believed to be somewhere between two and five weeks.[3] This means that if 60% of people are aware of an advert immediately after it's been aired, this will reduce to 30% within just a few weeks.

And that figure is for adverts – which are usually designed to be emotive and memorable! For the typical office email, Facebook update or company pitch, the memory half-life is probably much shorter than two-to-five weeks. I can think of a few PowerPoint presentations I'd forgotten before they were even finished . . .

A review of early studies on memory decay produced the chart shown below, showing recall over a logarithmic scale of minutes – for things less engaging than adverts, the memory 'half-life' appears to be much shorter than a few weeks, although for very engaging content, like poems, the 'half-life' is much longer.[4]

The exponential rate of forgetting for different types of stimulus

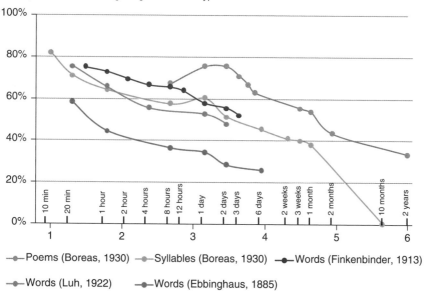

—●—Poems (Boreas, 1930) —●—Syllables (Boreas, 1930) —●—Words (Finkenbinder, 1913)

—●—Words (Luh, 1922) —●—Words (Ebbinghaus, 1885)

It is little wonder therefore that research demonstrates a positive relationship between message memorability and behavioural effectiveness.[5] No matter how strong a 'nudge' a message gives, that 'nudge' generally needs to be remembered in order to work.

So, the first way to make sure a message influences action, then, is to make sure it gets remembered.

10 MEMORY

To put it simply, an awful lot of stuff happens in the world every day, yet only a very select few things are remembered on a large scale. Everybody can recall, for example, where they were when Kennedy got shot, or when the Twin Towers came down – as the old cliché goes.

Why is it that certain things are much more memorable than others? More importantly, does it matter?

Firstly, memorability does indeed matter. As discussed earlier, a message has to be remembered if it is to have its desired effects after some time; not only that, however, but the more mentally salient, or front-of-mind, a message is, the more likely it is to influence behaviour.

Researchers illustrated this point with an experiment in which participants were asked to look through twenty pictures and rate them;[1] little did they realise that some of the pictures subtly contained a bottle of Dasani-branded water. After the picture task, participants were offered their choice of bottled water from a selection of four brands. As illustrated in the chart below, simply putting a thought to the front of people's minds can be enough to influence their behaviour in its favour.

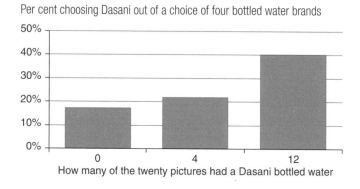

Per cent choosing Dasani out of a choice of four bottled water brands

How many of the twenty pictures had a Dasani bottled water

As for *why* some stimuli are better remembered than others, there are four basic principles.

ATTENTION OR PROCESSING

Firstly, as shown through experiments cited earlier in the book, primal, emotional, personal and surprising stimuli and more likely to be recalled. This is not only because we are more likely to even notice these types of stimuli, but also because we divert more attentional processes to them and endow them with deeper cognitive processing.[2] Similarly, because, as shown earlier, curiosity, narrative and fluency result in more efficient or enhanced cognitive processing, these types of stimuli are also more likely to be remembered.

Get a message attended to and thought about, and it will have a much better chance of being remembered!

REPETITION

'Education, education, education.'

This was Tony Blair's slogan on, yes, education in the run up to the 1997 election. It was so successful that it has been named as Blair's 'winning general election mantra' by one commentator,[3] with another speculating that it should be inscribed in the *Oxford Book of Quotations*.[4] The book *The Elements of Eloquence: How to Turn the Perfect English Phrase* is particularly laudatory, noting that it received the biggest round of applause and the most headlines of the Labour party conference.[5]

Part of the massive success of this mantra is ostensibly *repetition*: repetition is key for memory.

There is a huge amount of research to suggest this, that repetition is key for memory. To give just one illustration, American psychologist Benton Underwood presented his participants with a long list of two-syllable nouns, in which specific words had been repeated one, two, three or four times throughout the list; afterwards, participants wrote down as many words as they could recall.[6] There was a strong positive correlation between repetition and recall: only 27% of the words shown once were recalled, compared to 71% of the words shown four times.

Every time a message is repeated, that message's links in memory are refreshed and strengthened – as shown in the crude illustration below – making subsequent spontaneous remembering, or cue-based triggering, of a memory much more likely.

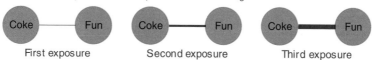

Effect on memory networks of exposures to the message that coke is fun

First exposure   Second exposure   Third exposure

From a message perspective, research has shown that increasing the frequency of message exposure enhances the likelihood of it being remembered – as one might expect.

An experiment conducted in the 1980s asked its participants to watch two half-hour TV shows with advertisements sandwiched in the 'breaks'; a week later, they did the same thing again and then completed various measures for each advert that was shown to them.[7] The adverts embedded in the total two-hour programming varied according to how many times they were repeated. As can be seen below, ad repetition had a positive impact on both recall and purchase intentions.

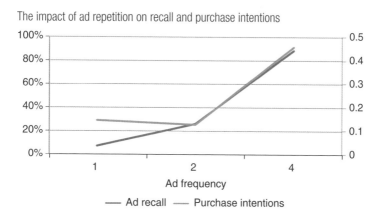

The impact of ad repetition on recall and purchase intentions

Ad frequency

—— Ad recall —— Purchase intentions

Similarly, a meta-analytic review looked at the effects of ad repetition and found the more a single advert was repeated, the increasingly negative attitudes towards the ad become; but ad repetition was still associated with an increase in recall and sales every time the ad was repeated.[8] Recall that the advert for HeadOn increased sales by over 200% in the year it was released, despite being very repetitive, and thus hated![9]

The meta-analysis did, however, find a different pattern of results for repeating a *series* of ads rather than one specific ad; in this case, attitudes became less positive but didn't become negative, while for recall and sales there was an exponential increase in line with repetition. It appears the combination of the familiar and the new – or repetition and surprise – via a consistent series of adverts is the best route.

A great example of this comes from ALDI, who, *Marketing* magazine report, was the best-performing brand in 2014 in terms of advertising recall.[10] Not only this, but the ad campaign propelled ALDI's market share from a standstill to a 43% growth on the previous year, produced a return on investment of 15:1, and delivered the biggest sales growth in ALDI's history.[11]

This success is likely due, at least in part, to ALDI's use of a highly repeated *series* of adverts which used consistent, repetitive elements (since repetition is key for memory) while continuing to be surprising and interesting. In every ad, a character would say, 'I like these . . . I also like these . . .' with one product being placed on the left of the screen and one on the right, with prices in yellow overlaid on both – seemingly drawing attention to ALDI's proposition of offering the same quality at lower prices. This format was unchanged, but the adverts featured everything from a topless hunk drinking two types of champagne to a squeaky-voiced muppet eating two types of Jaffa Cakes.

Interestingly, there is also evidence that the effects of repetition go beyond just memory to influence attitudes and persuasion as well. The illusion-of-truth effect refers to the finding that people are more likely to believe statements are true the more times they hear them.[12] One study showed participants a five-minute video of two youths breaking into a house and leading police on a car chase, and then participants were asked various questions about the video.[13] However, some of these questions subtly contained information that was not true: for example, 'At the beginning of the scene, a young man dressed in jeans, a T-shirt *and gloves* entered the house. Did he enter through the door?'

False statements such as the assertion that the boy was wearing gloves were inserted into the questioning a variable number of times, either zero, once or thrice. Later, participants were asked if items, such as the boy wearing gloves, were present in the video. When an item didn't appear in the questions at all, misattribution (i.e. those saying it was in the video) was at 10%. Meanwhile, 37% of the items mentioned once were wrongly thought to have been in the video, compared to 56% when an item was mentioned three times.

As Goebbels actually *didn't* say (ironically), 'Any lie told often enough becomes the truth.'

Ultimately, the point is that repetition is key for memory. I'll say it again: repetition is key for memory.

When crafting messages that stick, it is important to make sure the message is repeated as much as possible, and to make sure that they key points *within* the message are repeated – for example, via the rhetorical rule of three used so effectively by Tony Blair.

PRIMACY AND RECENCY

Stimuli placed at the beginning and end of an experience are most likely to be remembered.

This principle is known as 'the primacy and recency effect'.

To take an example, one study gave people twelve lists containing six words each, and, after each list, participants were asked to recall as many of the six words as they could. As can be seen in the data below, there is a recall benefit to being placed at the end of the list, and even more so at the beginning.[14]

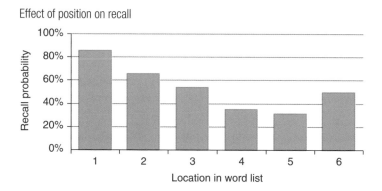

Effect of position on recall

The primacy effect is believed to occur because people have more time to absorb and rehearse the stimuli at the beginning than those which come after; and they are better able to remember these before the following stimuli becomes overwhelming and depletes their cognitive resources which would be used to process and remember the rest of the stimuli. Meanwhile, the recency effect is believed to occur because the last stimuli are still available in short-term memory after the list. This does however mean that the recency effect may not persist over time – that is to say, it's often short lived.

In a great example of this point, and of applying the primacy principle to message stickiness, social psychology pioneer Solomon Asch wrote two descriptions of a person, which were identical in the traits they described, except that the traits were in the reverse order.[15] One group read about a chap whose traits were described in order as intelligence, industry, impulsiveness, criticism, stubbornness, and envy; the other group read a description with the traits in the reverse order.

Among those who read the traits from intelligence to envy, 32% rated the person as happy, 74% as good-looking and 64% as restrained, among other things. Among those who read the traits in the opposite direction, 5% rated the person as happy, 35% as good-looking and 9% as restrained.

It seems that the perception of a message's content can be heavily influenced by what comes first!

However, there is in fact additional research supporting the existence of a long-term recency effect – such as the peak-end rule, which will be discussed next.

As well as carefully placing key content *within* a message, this principle can also be used when deciding where the message itself should sit: the first Tweet of a conference will probably be remembered better than all those which follow it during the day. As an illustration, research on radio ads found that 14% of people could correctly recognise an advert when it was played in a small block of one or two ads, but only 4% could when it was played in the middle of a large block of nine ads.[16]

This principle can be used to make messages stickier by placing the message at the beginning or end of an experience (for example, presenting a pitch at the beginning or end of a day's workshop, rather than in the middle). Furthermore, the principle can be used *within* messages, by making sure that the most important points are placed at the beginning or end of the communique; likewise, put the most important information at the start of sentences, slogans, headers and so on, rather than the middle.

To recap: stimuli placed at the beginning and end of an experience are the most likely to be remembered.

PEAK–END RULE

The final memory principle to consider here is 'the peak–end rule', which posits that both the end of an experience and its emotional peak will define how it is remembered.[17]

Celebrated behavioural scientist Daniel Kahneman co-authored some papers looking at the sexy world of colonoscopies. One of the papers found that patients' ratings of procedure discomfort were positively predicted by two factors: the maximum (peak) amount of pain the patients felt during the procedure; and the pain they felt in the final (end) moments of the procedure.[18]

Similar to the recency effect, the peak–end rule partly argues that people remember the end of an experience. Another of Kahneman's bum-camera studies randomly split patients into two groups: those who underwent the usual colonoscopy procedure; and those who underwent the normal procedure, but with the tube left in place for an additional three minutes in a way that was uncomfortable, but not painful.[19] The patients in the latter group retrospectively rated the experience as less unpleasant on the whole (so to speak), and they were more likely to return for further procedures; this is ostensibly because the end of the experience was less painful, despite the total procedure being prolonged.

Likewise, asked to do one of the following again, people would rather leave their hand in 14°C cold water for one minute followed by 15°C water for another than leave it in 14°C water for one minute only.[20] Of course, this is completely irrational – but the first condition was favoured because the end memory of the experience was less painful with the moderately cold water than the freezing water.

Interestingly, there is evidence indicating that people's voting behaviours are based on the actions of political parties in the election year rather than a comprehensive retrospective assessment – in other words, the most recent, or endmost, experience with politicians is what sways us.[21]

In terms of memory for the emotional peak of an event, we have already discussed at length why emotional things are well-remembered. A nice illustration comes from research on holidays: specifically, people's memories of holidays are primarily influenced by the most surprising or memorable day. We always look back on our holidays with fondness, generally forgetting the tedious plane rides, family arguments and spot of food poisoning.

When it comes to messages, then, it's important to make sure your key points aren't forgotten in favour or something more emotional or exciting in the message – and likewise, that the message itself isn't overwhelmed by more emotional surrounding stimuli. For example, a recent paper looked at the effectiveness of adverts sandwiched in between violent or sexual TV content.[22] As you can see, adverts are better remembered if they are surrounded by dull content.

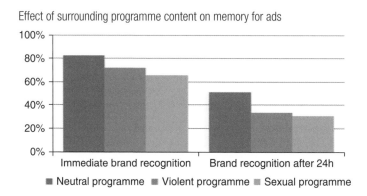

Effect of surrounding programme content on memory for ads

So get remembered – it's important! Make sure your messages are hooked in people's minds by using repetition (particularly by repeating certain elements while refreshing others), by positioning your messages at the start or end of an experience, and by making sure your messages are the emotional high-point of an experience.

And remember: repetition is key for memory!

SUMMARY

Memory

Do

✓ Recognise that memory plays a hugely vital part in influencing behaviour; 'getting in people's heads' is more important than influencing attitudes.

✓ Use emotion, personalisation, surprise, and so on to make messages more memorable.

✓ Make use of repetition, repetition, repetition – both for the message at a macro level and also within the message itself.

✓ Make sure the message (or, within the message, its key point) is the emotional peak.

Don't

✗ Forget (!) that people are exposed to countless messages each day, and that only a select few stick in memory.

✗ Be inconsistent in repeated messaging.

✗ Put messages in the middle of a context (or put the key points within the middle of the message itself); instead, use the beginning and the end.

✗ Make sure messages aren't crowded out by extreme emotions.

11 AUTOPILOT

I recently conducted an experiment with *Webs of Influence* author Nathalie Nahai, where we asked people to read a scenario and rate how likely they would be to behave in a certain way.[1] Imagine, for example . . .

> *You are in a different country for one evening on a business trip. For dinner, you can order something simple at the hotel, but you are thinking of going out to a restaurant. You are visiting a fairly small town in a developing country with a poor reputation for food hygiene. Having walked around for 20 minutes, you are thinking of giving up – but you then find two places where the food looks good.*
> *A. One of the restaurants is empty. You decide to look the restaurant up on an app on your smartphone, but you can't find any reviews.*
> *B. The other restaurant is extremely busy and there is a queue of people waiting at the door. You decide to look the restaurant up on an app on your smartphone, and you see that hundreds of people have visited the place and left reviews.*

Which restaurant would you choose?

Almost certainly you will have plumped for the second one. Our experiment found the same. Respondents were randomly assigned to one of two restaurants, and then rated on a scale of one to five how likely they would be to eat there.

People were a third more likely to eat at the restaurant if it was popular.

This is one of the most popular examples of a heuristic (i.e. a rule-of-thumb run on autopilot) – whether you would choose a busy, noisy restaurant to eat your dinner, or an empty, quiet one. Nearly everybody chooses the busy restaurant straight away: the thinking is ostensibly that if the restaurant is busy, the food must be good.

That is precisely what a heuristic is – a shortcut, or rule-of-thumb, that is used without thinking to make quick decisions that work. The vast majority of the time, the busy restaurant *will* be better and safer than the quiet restaurant; using the number of people as an instant shorthand is much quicker and easier than, for example, consciously and deliberatively reading the menu, looking for the restaurant's Food Standards Agency certificate, and looking at how clean the place is inside.

Remember, we have very limited brainpower to spend on decisions: for example, the best estimate (although it is still a crude estimate) is that we only process 0.0004% of sensory information consciously.[2] At the same time, there is a huge amount of complexity in the world: we are faced with over 200 decisions a day for food alone.[3]

We use heuristics in order to cope with all of this information and all of these decisions that need to be made, without having to expend limited time and energy. There is a strong evolutionary bent to heuristics, as shown by their existence in primates[4] – and even honeybees.[5]

There is a fascinating implication to heuristics being innately hardwired: it is very difficult, if not impossible, to 'outsmart' heuristics. In the same way that an optical illusion cannot be unseen, the effect of a heuristic cannot be avoided.

One paper reports how students at a top university in the States were given a 90-minute lecture on the bowl-size effect, where people eat more food from bigger bowls.[6] Six weeks later, they were invited to a Super Bowl party, where they were invited to help themselves to Chex Mix to nibble on while they watched the game. The Chex Mix was served from either two one-gallon bowls or four half-gallon bowls. Those who took Chex Mix from the larger bowls ate 59% more of the snack by the end of the party.

Other experiments have found that, even if people are warned specifically about a particular cognitive bias, the bias still occurs in subsequent tests![7]

Since Daniel Kahneman and Amos Tversky ignited interest in heuristics in the 1970s,[8] and especially since Thaler and Sunstein's *Nudge* entered the global consciousness,[9] the wealth of information on using heuristics to influence people has exploded. There have now been dozens and dozens of heuristics identified in research; however, the most appropriate framework for message stickiness is ostensibly Robert Cialdini's landmark book *Influence*,[10] which proposed six principles for persuasion: scarcity, authority, social proof, reciprocity, liking, and commitment and consistency.

SCARCITY

I'm going to tell you a secret (gents, don't tell your missus): diamonds are intrinsically worthless.

If you don't believe me, listen to what former chairman of De Beers diamond company, Nicky Oppenheimer, had to say:[11] 'Diamonds are intrinsically worthless . . .' (see http://www.independent.co.uk/life-style/the-gem-trail-diamonds-from-angolan-mine-to-third-finger-left-hand-1070530.html)

The truth is that De Beers, after essentially forming a diamond monopoly, restricted global supply of the jewels,[12] with the effect that the value of diamonds, and thus prices, rose significantly (see McConnell, C. R., and Brue, S. L. (2005). *Economics: Principles, Problems, and Policies* (pp. 456)). This happened because we are hardwired to want something more if it is scarce.

On the one hand, we value scarce things more because owning them transfers qualities of uniqueness and individuality to the owner,[13] and indicates that the owner has wealth and prestige.[14] On a much more fundamental level than that, however, there is a strong evolutionary component to valuing scarce goods, namely that it drives us to stockpile things that need to be stockpiled. Research has shown, for example, that signals of food scarcity cause animals to value food more and be more competitive with one another over it;[15] similarly, researchers have demonstrated a clear relationship between countries' and regions' levels of deprivation and their rates of violent behaviour.[16]

For one experiment, researchers invited their participants to sit down and sample the goods placed in front of them – namely a pack of cigars, a can of mints, and a glass jar of cookies – having been told that only a small number of people were participating overall.[17] Then, the participants rated each item on several dimensions. Except, the twist is that the cookie jar was randomly assigned to contain either two or ten cookies. The participants' ratings of liking and attraction, standardised to a percentage, and their estimates of the cookies cost per pound, are shown in the chart below: all three are increased by perceived scarcity.

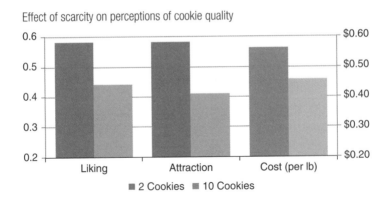

Effect of scarcity on perceptions of cookie quality

In terms of making messages sticky, using scarcity to increase the perceived urgency or value of a message's desired behaviour can enhance the likelihood of it being carried out.

txt2stop was a mobile-based smoking cessation programme which used behavioural science 'nudges', sent via text message, to help people stop smoking; an experiment showed that abstinence after six months was significantly higher among people who participated in the programme than among controls.[18] But how could you get people to participate?

People were initially invited to register their interest in txt2stop by texting a number found in adverts, GP surgeries, and so on; after doing so, these people are given information on the programme and then invited to consent to take part. In June 2009, txt2stop had a database of almost 2,000 people who had shown interest but had not followed up by consent to participate. Half of these potential users were sent a text message reminding them that they could text back to consent to join: 6.9% of them consented.[19]

The other half, however, were sent the same message with the following addition: 'Join txt2stop – only 300 places left!'

10.1% consented – or 1.5 times as many in the control group, a significant difference.

(As a side note, with this principle, and others, it's important to be cognisant of local law – and ethical considerations. When using a scarcity claim for the number of places left on a course, for example, you may need to make sure the course places are *actually* restricted. The Competition and Marketing Authority in the UK has been cracking down on sneaky psychological influences like this.[20] It's fine to nudge, but be lawful and ethical.)

EXERCISE

Reframing with scarcity

Rewrite the following sentence, or add to it, in order to use scarcity to make it more persuasive:

Sandals now on sale for half price.

SOCIAL PROOF

If all your friends jumped off a bridge, would you do it too? Actually, you very well might do.

Imagine you're walking down the street, and you notice a group of people standing there staring up at the sky; there doesn't seem to be anything there but a lot of people are looking. Would you stop to look?

Influential social psychologist Stanley Milgram published a paper in 1969 looking at this very thing.[21] Milgram corralled a group of researchers onto a New York street and had them nonchalantly mingle with the passing pedestrians; at a given, discreet signal, the group stood together and stared for a minute at a building's sixth-floor window – where nothing was actually happening. During this time the street was filmed, so that a pair of judges could count how many of the total 1,424 passers-by stopped and how many looked up at the window.

The key to the study was that groups of different sizes were tested. When one man alone was looking up, only 4% of people stopped – but with a group of 15, this rose to 40% of people.

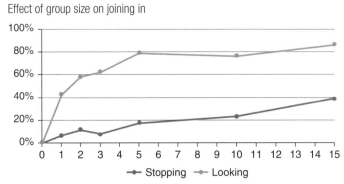

Effect of group size on joining in

Source: Adapted from Milgram, S., Bickman, L. and Berkowitz, L. (1969). 'An note on the drawing power of crowds of different size', Journal of Personality and Psychology, 13(2), 78–82.

This is the social proof heuristic – the rule-of-thumb which says, 'If everyone else is doing it, it must be good.'

This is why, to give an example, you rarely see discarded newspapers on their own around London Underground: instead, they seem to gather together in certain places, like the bottom of the escalator. In fact, a study was co-authored by Cialdini in which unknowing participants were discretely observed as they returned to their car, where researchers had placed a leaflet on their windshield for half of the participants, a person walked past at that time and picked up a piece of litter, while for the other half, the person walked past but didn't pick anything up. In the latter instance, 39% of people dropped the leaflet on the floor; however, when the social norm of environmental responsibility was activated by a person picking up a piece of rubbish, only 18% littered.[22]

Social proof is adaptive. Not only does it aid social interactions and hierarchies, but it provides an instant barometer of what is good and safe to do: if everybody eats the red berries, I can eat the red berries; if everyone avoids the dark cave, I would do well to avoid it; and if everyone is running in the opposite direction, I should probably run too.

For communications, social proof helps to make messages sticky by implicitly encouraging audiences that the target behaviour is the correct course of action to take.

Imagine, for example, that you own a public radio station that depends on fundraising to keep afloat. During an on-air fund drive, the DJ will play clips appealing for donations in between the pop songs and the witty banter. When listeners phone in, one of the production staff answers with the following prepared message: 'Hello, CPN member line. Are you a new member or a renewing member of CPN? How much would you like to pledge today?'

Researchers found that the addition of just seven words to this script increased donations by 12%, with the average donation rising from $106.72 to $119.70. What do you think these seven words might have been?[23]

'We had another member, they contributed $300.'

Or imagine that you work at Her Majesty's Revenue and Customs and you want to make sure everyone pays their taxes on time. If you want to increase the proportion filing their tax return on time, what single sentence might you add to the letters reminding people to do so?[24]

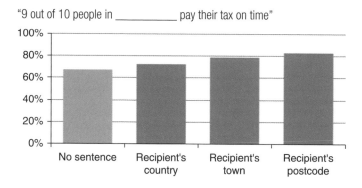

"9 out of 10 people in _____ pay their tax on time"

Reframing with social proof

Rewrite the following sentence, or add to it, in order to use social proof to make it more persuasive:

Come to Bognor Regis and enjoy the sunshine this Easter.

AUTHORITY

Stanley Milgram conducted another seminal experiment – you may be familiar with it.[25] Forty men participated in what they thought was a test of learning and memory: each was told to take the role of a 'teacher' while another participant, unseen and communicating over intercom, was to be the 'learner'. Adhering to the instructions of a researcher in a lab coat, the 'teacher' read out questions to test the memory of the 'learner'; if an answer was incorrect, the 'teacher' administered an electric shock. The first shock was 15v, and subsequent shocks increased by 15v each time.

Actually, the 'learner' was an actor who wasn't being shocked and who had rehearsed his reactions: 75v shocks (and up) elicited a grunt; from 120v to 345v, responses increased in intensity from complaints, to screams, to hysterically demanding to stop; he was silent from 345v onwards.

Milgram counted how many participants continued up to the highest shock possible, 450v, despite the person's screams and eerie silence (for reference, 100v can be fatal[35]): 65% did so.

Later, Milgram repeated this experiment with a twist: the researcher instructing the participants was *not* wearing a white lab coat, and the experiment was held in a run-down office rather than a university. In this context, fewer people (48%) administered the full 450v.

The conclusion is that we often instinctively obey authority figures. The white lab coat and the university setting acted as signals of legitimacy and authority, which increased compliance with what was clearly an abhorrent request.

Authority is the rule-of-thumb which says, 'If an expert has told me, it must be true'.

Since Milgram's studies, a lot of research has shown how authority signals can influence social compliance. One experiment featured: a blue-collar worker who was unshaven and wearing dirty old work clothes and a baseball hat; a businessman who was clean shaven with a suit and tie; or a fireman who wore, among other things, a blue shirt with a fire department patch on the sleeve.[26] The three types of men approached people on a street in Salt Lake City, pointed at another actor, and demanded, 'This fellow is over-parked at the meter but doesn't have any change. Give him a dime!'

44% of people complied with the blue-collar worker, and 50% with the businessman. However, an enormous 82% complied with the fireman, suggesting that a uniform is more persuasive than signals of high social status.

But what does this mean for messages?

Firstly, the perceived authority of a message's sender has a profound effect on persuasiveness. In fact, a meta-analysis found credibility to be the most important source characteristic for persuasion.[27] A single expert's publication in *The New York Times*,[28] or broadcast on national TV,[29] can change public opinion on policy issues by up to 4%.

Ergo, subtle cues like title and profession can be used in messages to make them more effective. For example, mothers bringing their child to a school psychologist for a test were informed of a relevant book on child development; when the psychologist introduced himself as 'Mr', none of the parents sent off for the book, but 17% did so when he introduced himself as a doctor.[30] Similarly, sending off to receive a free booklet on dental care was influenced by the job title of the person suggesting it:[31]

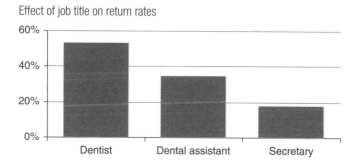

Effect of job title on return rates

If, however, as a sender you are personally lacking in authority, it's always possible to borrow some from someone else. One experiment discovered that accompanying a picture of an object with a picture of a relevant celebrity expert – such as a sports shoe with Andre Agassi – increased favourable attitudes towards the object by 12% and recognition memory by 10%.[32]

Furthermore, persuasiveness can be increased through authoritative communicating. For example, a salesperson trying to sell a cleaning device for an eight-track tape player (it was the 1970s . . .) was successful 22% of the time when their spiel included, 'Here is a thing we have on special that they tell me will keep your tape player clean,' and 67% of the time when it included 'Here is a device we have on special that will clean the dirt and tape oxide from the guides, the head, and especially the drive wheels of your tape player.'[33]

Though making messages authoritative can be more subtle than this. A study used real court transcripts to simulate a witness being questioned, in which the witness' language made them out to be either powerful or powerless.[34] Powerful speech contained more intensifiers (e.g. 'definitely'), hedges (e.g. 'kind of'), questions, gestures, uses of 'sir', and dropped consonants (e.g. 'jus' now'), and fewer one-word answers. Participant ratings showed that witnesses using powerful language were rated as more credible; and a different paper found the same thing for ads.[35]

In the end, adding authority to your message can increase compliance by making the request appear to be the sensible thing to do – even if that request is to murder with electricity!

Reframing with authority

Rewrite the following sentence, or add to it, in order to use authority to make it more persuasive:

Toast on jam tastes better with Lurpak butter.

RECIPROCITY

Think back to last Christmas. Did you receive any presents which ended up in the cupboard, down the charity shop, in the bin, or rewrapped for someone else? Perhaps a pair of goofy Simpsons socks, a head-massager, or cheap perfume?

To put it kindly, we tend to buy a lot of pointless, worthless tat at Christmas. A popular gift of recent years has been 'The Useless Box' – a nondescript black box with a single switch, which, when pushed on, activates a robotic arm which pops out of the box and pushes the switch back off.

These gifts might seem fun and harmless, but the situation goes from 'ho, ho, ho' to 'bah humbug' when we actually look at the figures: one report estimated that Brits waste over £2 billion on unwanted Christmas gifts every year.[36]

So why do we act so irrationally at Christmas? Why do we buy presents that we *know* people don't want?

To answer this, we need to first turn to a Christmas-themed experiment published in 1976.[37] Sociologists Phillip Kunz and Michael Woolcott bought almost 600 Christmas cards and sent them to inhabitants of Midwestern America selected at random from *Polk Directories.* To emphasise, these recipients were chosen completely at random and had no relation to the researcher who signed and sent the card.

One in five people sent a Christmas card back.

The principle at play here is reciprocity – a deeply hardwired heuristic which says, 'If somebody has helped me, I will help them in return.'

Reciprocity is a powerful motivator because it's so key to who we are as a species. Humans are very social animals who have evolved to live in groups and survive by cooperating with one another; if all (or most) of a group's members were freeloaders, taking from the group without giving back, the social group could not function.[38]

As with other principles, the innate nature of reciprocity is demonstrated by its existence in our primate relatives. Researchers conducted a meta-analysis of social grooming among primates and found that reciprocity explained 20% of why monkeys groom, while familial relatedness explained only 3%.[39] To put it another way, when it comes to primate nit-picking, 'I'll scratch your back if you scratch mine' is more important than 'being a monkey's uncle'.

In fact, reciprocity is so hardwired that it's even practiced by a species of dance fly known as *Rhamphomyia sulcata*.[40] In their experiment, researchers at the University of St Andrews intercepted some male fruit flies and replaced the food they were carrying with a piece of cotton. The male flies were using the food as a form of gift-exchange with females: they would offer the food and get some hot fly-on-fly action in return. But interestingly, the flies copulated for the same amount of time even if the gift was the inedible fluff; it was the gift exchange, not the gift itself, which was important and resulted in reciprocal copulation.

Incidentally, 88% of men buy their partner gifts for Valentine's Day,[41] and the most popular gifts include plush toys, chocolates, cards and flowers[42] (worthless fluff, then); and a quarter of men explicitly expect a bit of you-know-what in exchange for their gift.[43] Fortunately for them, one study found that women rated a higher likelihood of giving their number to a man, going on a date with him, and having sex with him, if he bought her a drink.[44]

More generally though, many, many papers have been published demonstrating the power of reciprocity on compliance. To give one example, one such paper describes a study in which a participant is seated in a room with another participant (who is actually a stooge) to complete a survey.[45] At one point the stooge left the room to visit a vending machine, and returned with two Coca-Colas – one for himself, and one as a gift for the participant. After the surveys were finished, the stooge asked the participant for a favour: he had to rush somewhere now, but he also had to deliver this important letter to the Controller's Office within the next 20 minutes; the office is only five minutes away, so perhaps the participant wouldn't mind taking it for him?

The soda gift increased compliance from 66% to a massive 94%.

In terms of communication, the insight is clear: give people a gift and they'll be more likely to comply with the message's request.

For example, the likelihood that a person will fill out and return a survey has been found to be increased from 10% to 30% by giving him or her a free bottle of water;[46] and research suggests that people will be 50% more likely to help with answering a survey if a $1 bill is included.[47]

Reciprocity doesn't have to be costly, though. An online study, for example, found that website visitors were more likely to give away their contact details if the website gave them a free download beforehand;[48] and research on tipping in service industries has found that tips can be increased through reciprocity using gifts as simple as a puzzle,[49] a compliment[50] or a drawing of a smiley face.[51]

Ultimately, we feel a strong urge to repay social debts, no matter how small, and this can be a powerful technique for message stickiness.

EXERCISE

Reframing with reciprocity

Rewrite the following sentence, or add to it, in order to use reciprocity to make it more persuasive:

Your local authority needs your help volunteering to help the elderly.

LIKING

One sunny June evening in 1994, a nondescript white Ford Bronco was cruising through the streets of Los Angeles at a leisurely 35 miles per hour. Several police cars trailed behind with their sirens blaring, as news helicopters thundered above. This was of course OJ Simpson's nationally televised slow-speed chase before his trial for the murder of his ex-wife Nicole Brown and her friend Ronald Goldman.

To state some facts of the case (see http://en.wikipedia.org/wiki/O.J.Simpson_murder_case):[52] Simpson owned a pair of gloves holding his DNA, with one of the pair being found at the crime scene and the other testing positive for Goldman's blood and being found in a bush on Simpson's estate, near where a house guest reported hearing movements around the time of the murder; before his car chase, Simpson wrote what was most likely a suicide letter, signing off, 'Don't feel sorry for me. I've had a great life, great friends. Please think of the real O.J. and not this lost person'.

Whatever did happen that day, one would infer that the evidence, rightly or wrongly, would be against Simpson and that he would be found guilty; yet, he was acquitted. Why?

In 1920, noted psychologist Edward Thorndike published a paper in which he first coined the term 'the halo effect' to refer to his finding that perceptions of individuals' different traits were strongly connected.[53] Thorndike asked military officers to rate their subordinate soldiers on a range of physical, cognitive and personal traits, and he showed that the ratings were strongly and positively correlated. For example, ratings of physique correlated with those of intellect at 0.31, leadership at 0.39 and character at 0.28. The halo effect essentially posits that a person viewed favourably in one sense is likely to have a halo around them, in that they are also viewed favourably in most every other sense.

In other words, if a person is rich, famous and beautiful, they are more likely to be perceived as trustworthy, honest and innocent. Indeed, there is research showing that attractive criminal defendants are more likely to be found not guilty and receive lighter punishments.[54]

In fact, attractive people have it very easy in life. The most attractive people enjoy an earnings premium of 5%, while the homeliest people suffer from an earnings penalty of 7–9%, for instance;[55] attractive people are more likely to be successful in job interviews as well.[56] In fact, beautiful people are just happier[57] and healthier[58] in general.

Similarly, with respect to compliance, a study on charitable giving found that blondes have more funds – that is, brunette women fundraisers raised an average of $1.31 from the passers-by they interacted with, while blondes raised an average of $2.42.[59]

Liking is not all about attractiveness, though. For instance, when an experimenter in one study mimicked the body language of the subject, the subject was 36% more likely to help pick up pens which were 'dropped', and 34% more likely to donate to the experimenter's charity.[60] Other studies have found that people are more likely to give someone a dime for the phone box if the two are dressed similarly,[61] and that people are 22% more likely to agree to read someone's eight-page essay and write a page of feedback on it if the two have simply small-talked for two minutes![62]

Overall, the essence of the liking heuristic is 'If I like it, or if it's good, it must be good'. That is, if a message or its sender are attractive, similar, familiar, or otherwise positively evaluated, it is more likely to be persuasive.

Imagine, for example, that you have a survey you would like people to fill in – oh, and, the survey is eight pages long and comprises 150 questions. What might you do to make people more likely to complete it?

Professor of Behavioural Sciences Randy Garner was faced with this very problem.[63] Some of the intended recipients of the survey were simply given an envelope stuffed with the questionnaire; while others were given the envelope with a Post-it note on top containing the handwritten message 'Please take a few minutes to complete this for us', with the personalised message ostensibly being a nice route to liking.

A third group, however, received the same Post-it note message, but signed, 'Thank you! R.G.'

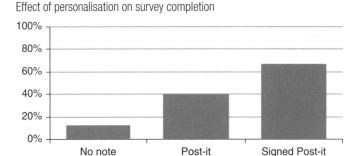

Effect of personalisation on survey completion

As can be seen in the chart, a more likeable message resulted in significantly higher compliance. Similarly, the South African payday loan paper mentioned earlier in this book found that, for male recipients of the letters, including a picture of a smiling woman increased loan take-up to the same degree as slashing the loan's interest rate by 4.5%;[64] and the click-through rates for charity emails were increased in one study from 4% to 22% simply by having the email sender's first name match that of the recipient.[65]

In sum, the efficacy of a message can be enhanced by making the message, its content or its sender more likeable.

EXERCISE

Reframing with liking

Rewrite the following sentence, or add to it, in order to use liking to make it more persuasive:

A vote for David Cameron is a vote for a Great Britain.

COMMITMENT AND CONSISTENCY

In May 2010, Conservative Party leader David Cameron formed a coalition government with the Liberal Democrats, headed by Nick Clegg. The Liberal Democrats won 23% of the vote in the general election, which, for the third party in a two-party system, was rather impressive, considering Labour won 29% of the vote.[66]

Overall, Nick Clegg was a funky, likeable guy who stood up for issues people cared about – for instance, he pledged that, should his party get into Government, they would abolish university tuition fees[67] (see http://news.bbc.co.uk/1/hi/uk_politics/8421092.stm).

When his party got into Government, they tripled tuition fees[68] (see http://www.bbc.co.uk/news/uk-politics-11803719).

While the Liberal Democrats won 24% of the vote in May 2010, this fell by a factor of three (ironically) to 8% of the vote in May 2015.[69]

People hate inconsistency. Psychological research has shown, for example, that people will feel giddy with schadenfreude if they catch someone doing an immoral act which that person had previously criticised others for doing.[70] As social animals we feel a strong urge to be seen to be consistent and reliable.

More than that, however, a principle called 'cognitive dissonance' is at play. Social psychologist Leon Festinger proposed cognitive dissonance as the unpleasant sense of tension or dissatisfaction created internally when two contrasting points are held to be true – and this internal discord works as a motivator to act in a way as to resolve the tension.[71]

For example, one experiment presented students with ten scenarios where people had cheated, such as secretly copying answers from a book during a test, and asked them to rate how severely the cheater should be punished.[72] Then, the students completed some tests – but some of them had the opportunity to cheat by, for example, marking their own answers. Afterwards, they completed another survey of attitudes towards cheating. Those who had cheated in the test subsequently had lower perceptions of punishment severity for cheaters. In this case, the cheaters' previous attitudes, that cheating should be punished severely, were inconsistent with their behaviours, that is, cheating; as a result, their attitudes had to change in order to match their actions and restore internal harmony.

The takeaway is that it is important for people to maintain a coherent sense of self and identity, and therefore they will act in a way that is consistent with their beliefs, behaviours and prior commitments. This is the 'commitment and consistency' heuristic: 'If I have committed to something, or it is consistent with who I am, I will do it.'

Therefore, messages' stickiness can be enhanced by either inferring that the message's desired action is consistent with the audience's identity, or by getting the audience to commit to the message's desired action in some way.

On the first point, one study found that, when people received manipulated feedback that they were the type of person who made environmentally friendly purchase decisions, they were consequently more likely to choose the more environmental product out of a choice of two.[73] Therefore, a message can encourage people to behave a certain way by implying that it is how they *would* normally behave.

On the second point, a piece of research in the States had Boy Scouts travel from door to door as part of a recycling awareness campaign.[74] In order to induce a commitment, some of the households were given an 'I Recycle to Win the War on Waste' sticker, and asked to sign a pledge on a piece of card that read, 'I, _____, pledge support for Claremont's Recycling Program. I will help win the war on waste!'

Every week for the following six weeks, a researcher noted for each household whether they had placed their recyclables at the front of their house. Among those in the control group, who didn't make a commitment to recycling, 11% began recycling in the six-week period. However, 42% of those who had made a commitment were ultimately recognised as recyclers.

The perception of commitment can also be artificially engineered. Two American researchers collaborated with a car wash in a major conurbation, where 300 customers were given a loyalty card that allowed them to enjoy a free car wash if they collected enough stamps.[75] Half of these customers were given a loyalty card requiring eight stamps to be filled in; the other half were given a loyalty card requiring ten stamps, but the first two had already been filled in, meaning that, again, only eight were actually needed. The second type of card, however, induced feelings of commitment by suggesting that 20% of the card had already been completed; as can be seen below, this was significantly more effective.

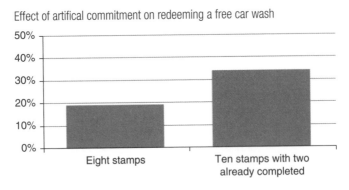

Effect of artifical commitment on redeeming a free car wash

A powerful technique that uses both commitment and consistency is something known as 'the foot-in-the-door technique', where people are more likely to agree to a large request if they agreed to a smaller one beforehand: for instance, people are more inclined to host a charitable cause's big, ugly sign on their lawn if they had previously agreed to take a small bumper sticker.[76] Similarly, survey completion rates are higher for people who are called before being sent the survey.[77]

Finally, another wonderful, but somewhat sneaky, principle is 'the mere agreement effect', where simply having people agree to a series of unrelated questions (i.e. 'Yes, yes, yes . . .') makes them significantly more likely to agree to a subsequent request for, say, a donation.[78] Therefore, people can be encouraged to act a certain way by having them just say, 'Yes', to preceding – even unrelated – questions.

In the end, if you want your audience to be more likely to act as a message intended, a useful tool can be to imply that acting in this way is in line with the audience's prior beliefs or behaviours.

EXERCISE

Reframing with commitment and consistency

Rewrite the following sentence, or add to it, in order to use commitment and consistency to make it more persuasive:

We are hosting a BBQ this weekend and would like you to come.

SUMMARY

Autopilot

Do

✓ Realise that most decisions are made on the basis of quick shortcuts.

✓ Use an intelligent understanding of heuristics to 'nudge' the behaviour of message recipients.

✓ Use scarcity signals to make a desired behaviour seem more urgent.

✓ Be liked, whether this is through attractiveness or similarity.

✓ Ask recipients to commit, or signal that they have committed, so they are more likely to act in a way that is consistent with the commitment.

✓ Give small (or even free) gifts to recipients.

✓ Use authority signals to make messages seem more credible and proper.

✓ Imply that everyone else is doing the behaviour you wish your recipients to do.

Don't

✗ Think that people can 'outsmart' heuristics: they are just like optical illusions which cannot be 'unseen'.

✗ Be unlawful or unethical in your use of influence tactics.

12 PRIMING

There is a significant proportion of the population who have rather large suspicions that Disney is trying to sneak subliminal messages about sex into their children's movies – if it's anything to go by, the video 'Disney Subliminal Messages' (uploaded by TheKilluminati786, no less) has, as of writing, almost 1.7 million views[1] (see https://www.youtube.com/watch?v=meHsuA0b1uE).

The topic has received so much attention that even major media agencies have addressed it,[2] finding that Disney has a rational explanation for everything (although, I suppose they *would* . . .): no, the magic dust in *The Lion King* doesn't spell 'SEX', it spells 'SFX'; no, the bishop in *The Little Mermaid* doesn't have an erection, it's just his knees; but yes, Jessica Rabbit was without underwear for a few frames in *Who Killed Roger Rabbit?*.

This is perhaps more of an indication of our hardwired tendency to look for patterns than any real sex-kitten mind-programming global conspiracy (*perhaps*), but it does raise an interesting point about the general public's fear of corporate subliminal manipulation. One survey, for example, found that 62% of respondents believed that advertisers were using subliminal manipulation on them.[3]

In 1957, a private market researcher named James Vicary caused outrage when he claimed to have increased a cinema's popcorn sales by over 50%, and its Coca-Cola sales by 18%, by subliminally flashing messages such as 'Eat Popcorn' throughout the cinema's films.[4] The study was cited in Packard's *The Hidden Persuaders* – a book which, at the height of the Cold War, claimed that consumers were powerless to marketers' nefarious techniques.[5] The idea that consumers could be so easily controlled and manipulated has proved abhorrent to a society which believes in free will and personal responsibility – so much so, that subliminal advertising was banned in countries like the UK and the US.

However, subsequent research has found that Vicary's study appears to have been a hoax for publicity; the experiment he claimed to have conducted has never been successfully replicated and subliminal advertising's effects have been found to be weak.[6]

So, is subliminal mind control possible? Are we living in an Orwellian dystopia, or is it all a load of old nonsense?

Well, there is some experimental evidence in favour of Vicary's 'Eat Popcorn' claim to at least some degree. Researchers from Lancaster University got 112 children aged between 6 and 12 to sit down at school and watch a bit of TV: specifically, they were shown a two-minute clip from the children's classic *Home Alone*.[7] Afterwards, the children were randomly taken one-by-one into a room separate from the classroom, where the researcher asked them a few simple questions. Before the questioning though, the children were each offered a free drink of their choice between Coke and Pepsi.

Half of the children watched a segment from *Home Alone* in which the family was shown eating dinner, with Pepsi featuring quite heavily; the other half saw a clip which was similar in theme and content, but featured milk instead of Pepsi. 42% of the children who saw the milk clip chose Pepsi over Coke, whereas, among the viewers of the Pepsi clip, 62% chose Pepsi. Interestingly, whether or not the children could recall having seen Pepsi did not affect their choice.

Exposure to a Pepsi stimulus did in fact increase the consumption of Pepsi, giving credence to Vicary's assertion that 'Drink Coca-Cola' would increase Coca-Cola sales.

Another experiment addressed Vicary's claim more explicitly. In 'Beyond Vicary's fantasies: the impact of subliminal priming and brand choice', Dutch psychologists asked their participants to complete a timed word task.[8] In this task, subjects were shown a string of nine Bs (i.e. BBBBBBBBB) for 300ms, several times, except the strings sometimes contained a small B at a random point (e.g. BBbBBBBBB); subjects had to count how many of the strings contained a small B.

The sneaky part is that some words were flashed for just 23ms – that is, below conscious perception – before each B-string. For half of the participants, this non-conscious word stimulus was 'Lipton Ice'; for others it was a nonsense phrase using the same letters, like 'Npeic Tol'. A second key point is that half of the participants in each of these groups had to chew on a very salty sweet for a minute before the experiment began, ostensibly making them thirsty. Finally, participants were asked how likely they would be to select Lipton Ice over Coca-Cola or Spa Rood if they were offered the choice.

The effect of priming on proportion choosing Lipton Ice Tea over competitors

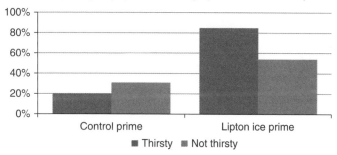

Control prime   Lipton ice prime
■ Thirsty ■ Not thirsty

The results, shown in the above chart, tell us two things. Firstly, choosing Lipton Ice could only be significantly subliminally influenced when participants were thirsty; the authors concluded that *goals* cannot be subliminally manipulated, but the *solutions* to those goals can. This is an important point which will be addressed later – namely, subliminal persuasion may only work in certain conditions. The second implication is that there is, again, support for Vicary's idea that brand purchases can be subliminally influenced.

Looking at these two studies alone, it is clear that subliminal advertising *may* actually work. Specifically, what these studies show is that making something mentally salient – that is, essentially reminding people of something, or putting it into their minds – can subsequently influence behaviour. This has been demonstrated earlier in the book where, for example, seeing orange Halloween decorations makes people more likely to think of orange brands like Sunkist,[9] or seeing chocolates on your work desk makes you more likely to eat them.[10]

This principle is known as 'priming', which refers to the process wherein exposure to a stimulus activates that stimulus' memory node in the brain, and consequently those memory nodes attached to it. To illustrate, the word 'priming' was first used in its contemporary meaning to explain why people who were given a list of words to memorise, and then asked to think up a spontaneous list of words, tended to include those words they had memorised, indicating those words were still active in memory from earlier.[11]

In the diagram below, as a very crude illustration, seeing a chair consequently activates, or 'primes', the construct of a chair in memory. To a lesser extent, this also activates memory nodes connected to the chair node, such as a table, or the behaviour of sitting down. It might therefore be hypothesised from this crude example that flashing images of a chair below conscious awareness could make people more likely to sit down than stand up.

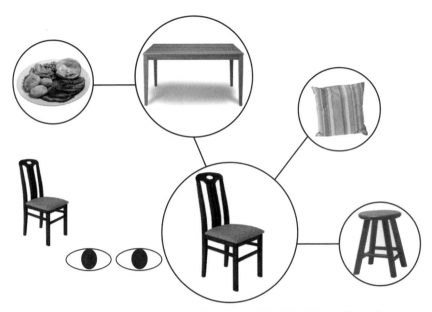

Sources: © Baloncici (cushion); © Joe Gough (dinner plate); © Horiyan (table); © DJ Srki (chair); © Joey Chan (stool)

There have been some fantastic papers published demonstrating how priming can influence behaviour in surprising ways. In perhaps the most well-known example, social psychologist John Bargh and colleagues instructed participants to solve 30 scrambled five-word sentences by turning them into coherent four-word sentences.[12] For example, 'they her send see usually' becomes 'they usually see her'. For half of the participants, the sentences were all relatively neutral; for the other half however, half of the sentences contained words related to the elderly, like 'wrinkled', 'grey' and 'Florida'. Once they were finished, the participants left – but, sneakily, a researcher used a stopwatch to time them as they walked away down a 9.75m corridor.

The participants who read words related to the elderly took, on average, 13% longer to walk away!

Another nice example comes from an experiment where participants answered a general knowledge quiz made up of 42 Trivial Pursuit questions.[13] Some of the participants dived straight into the quiz – others, however, had to spend five minutes beforehand imagining a typical professor and writing down all the attributes, appearances and behaviours that came into their minds, while the remaining third did the same for secretaries. The control group scored an average of 50%, while those who thought of professors scored 60% – something as seemingly unmalleable as crystallised intelligence appeared to be susceptible to priming.

There are many, many other cool and sexy examples of priming – like, for example, the finding that seeing Apple's logo, compared to IBM's, makes you better at creative thinking.[14] However, there has been a big question mark hanging over priming research recently. Researchers have failed to replicate key experiments,[15] priming was found to be one of the least reliable of several psychological principles,[16] and a meta-analysis found the size of the effect of subliminal advertising on choice (r=0.0585) to be about the same as the size of the effect of aspirin consumption on heart attacks.[17]

As discussed earlier, part of this may be to do with moderating variables. Perhaps the largest factor is the difference between subliminal and supraliminal priming: the latter involves more careful conscious processing of primes through, for example, unscrambling sentences or spending five minutes thinking about something; subliminal priming, meanwhile, involves incidental or non-conscious exposure to a stimulus. While supraliminal priming is more likely to achieve a result[18] (since it results in more cognitive processing), it is often infeasible in the real world.

Having said that, there are many studies which demonstrate that priming may be usable within messages for driving audience behaviour. For example, one experiment created a mock e-commerce website selling sofas;[19] however, what visitors to the site didn't realise was that the site's background was randomly assigned to be either pennies on green, or clouds on blue. The former ostensibly primes thoughts of money, while the latter primes quality for sofas (i.e. comfort). With the clouds, 39% of visitors bought the cheapest sofa, compared to 49% for the pennies.

One last piece of research created an advert for a restaurant comprising a picture of the venue and a piece of text copy beneath it; then they estimated how much they would be willing to pay for dinner for two, including drinks and dessert.[20] Half of the participants read the following copy, and estimated they would be willing to pay $46.45 on average: 'Enjoy tonight. Say so long to everything else.'

However, when 'so long' was replaced with 'goodbye', this amount jumped to $56.29, because the homonym 'buy' had ostensibly primed them to spend more money.

Ultimately, a well-placed word, phrase or image in a message can influence behaviour by priming relevant thoughts, feelings or behaviours: if you want to create a poster to keep the office kitchen tidy, for example, putting a pair of eyes on the poster will make people behave more responsibly![21]

Priming people

You are presenting a PowerPoint deck to a group of potential clients. Think of a way you can prime them – either supraliminally through, say, a conscious exercise, or subliminally through, say, a subtly placed picture – in order to achieve each of the results below.

1 Get them to be more talkative and open

2 Get them to be more generous

3 Get them to be more creative in a group task

Priming

Do

✓ Know that, contrary to belief, a certain level of subliminal influence is accessible via particular methods.

✓ Use an intelligent understanding of environmental cues to prime useful thoughts, feelings and behaviours.

✓ Use supraliminal priming (e.g. reading several words) over subliminal priming (e.g. quickly seeing a picture) wherever possible, as the former is stronger.

Don't

✗ Overestimate the power of priming, as its effects are often weak and unreliable.

✗ Use the power of subliminal priming for 'evil'; also, it is important to be transparent.

✗ Simply throw any messages together 'willy-nilly'; as we have seen, the slightest change to a message can have a big effect on behaviour.

PART 3

PUTTING IT TO USE

I was once told a great story from the annals of workshop lore. At a workshop for a major FMCG brand on influencing consumer behaviour with heuristics, the following example 'nudge', taken, in fact, from Thaler and Sunstein's *Nudge* was presented:[1]

 Gents, is there anything worse than going into a lavatory and coming out with wet shoes? Whether you accidentally marked yourself as your own territory, or whether you had to slosh through the mess made by others, it's not a nice experience. Fortunately, there is a clever – and now extremely popular – 'nudge' which reduces splashback at urinals: a fly sticker. There is a certain point in a urinal where the potential for splashback is at its lowest; if you put a small sticker or etching of a fly there, mess is significantly reduced simply because men have an innate urge to aim for it. It's an amazing application of the principle of 'monkey see, monkey do'.

However, back at the workshop, one of the attendees raised his hand. 'That's great . . . But how does it help me sell yoghurts?'

The point is – to paraphrase a popular saying – knowledge without a practical application is useless.

So, in this final section of the book, we'll take the scientific principles outlined previously and explain how to use them in specific contexts – namely promotion, social media, direct mail and the workplace. We will give concrete, practical advice on how to hook people with these messages.

But first, the insights are recapped in a handy-reference toolkit for creating a sticky message.

YOUR KIT FOR CRAFTING THE PERFECT COMMUNICATION

Although it's something of a cliché, research suggests that men really don't like asking for help: for example, men are less likely to go to the doctor,[2] and when they do, they ask fewer questions,[3] a pattern which has serious repercussions for male health.[4] Likewise, although men are more likely to have substance abuse problems, they are less likely to seek help for it.[5]

The point of all this is that the following pneumonic acronym can be presented without it sounding a bit like Jerry Seinfeld:

Primal	Mystery	Memory
Affective	Ease	Autopilot
Self-relevant	Narrative	Priming
Surprising		

Every time you are crafting a message, just remember that, when you're lost, rather than asking them to ask for directions you should **pass men** a **map**.

Here is your communication toolkit for crafting the perfect communication; simply make sure you follow this process every time you want to create a sticky message.

1 INVITING ATTENTION

People are usually busy and distracted, and they have relatively limited attention spans; yet, there is an awful lot of information out there in the world. Will people even notice your message?

Make sure your message includes at least one of the items for the following checklist so that it can cut through the noise:

- **Primal** Does your message contain: images or words which relate to food, especially that which is high in calorific content; images or words which explicitly reference sex or which imply it through innuendo, or an image of a physically attractive person; or a face, no matter how simple and even including emoticons?

- **Affective** Does your message contain: words relating to emotion like 'love'; images of emotional faces; high-arousal words like swear words; baby-schema congruent stimuli like puppies, kittens or babies themselves; biologically threatening stimuli like snakes, spiders or sharks; or violence or the threat of violence; or any other stimuli which are emotionally arousing, whether good or bad?

- **Self-relevant** Does your message contain: information which is personal to the recipient, whether it's their face, their name, or even their first initial; first-person singular pronouns like 'me'; stimuli which are not personal but which will be at the front of many people's minds, like celebrities or seasonal references; or information which has been personalised to the recipient's personality or tastes?

- **Surprising** Does your message contain: noises, particularly loud noises; moving images, particularly with lots of movement or scene changes; stimuli that contrast with the surrounding environment in terms of colour, movement or sound; a stimulus that breaks established patterns or does not fit with mental predictions; something never seen before; or something that would not be expected in the message's context?

2 IGNITING THINKING

Getting noticed is just the first step: if people do not 'absorb' your message then they won't remember it and it won't influence their thoughts and behaviours.

In order to be cognitively processed, and thus have an effect in the minds of recipients, your message must use at least one of the following checklist items:

- **Mystery** Does your message contain: a puzzle or riddle for recipients to solve; something which does not immediately make sense or which does not have an immediately clear answer; just enough missing information to leave people wanting more; a question; or an engaging metaphor?

- **Ease** Does your message: keep itself as short as possible; use simple, concrete words; use images wherever possible; use smart design to make the key points as easy to realise as possible; demand very little of its audience; or make things as easy as possible for people by suggesting what to do?

- **Narrative** Does your message contain a story comprising a clear protagonist who has a goal and sets out to achieve it along a clear narrative arc comprising an initial exposition, a beginning where a tension is introduced, a middle where the character sets out to resolve the tension, and an end where the tension is somehow resolved?

▶

3 INCITING ACTION

A message being noticed and processed will be more effective than others – however, its ability, once absorbed, to influence behaviour can be enhanced.

Make sure your message uses memory in order to influence behaviour further down the line:

- **Memory** Does your message: use repetition to emphasise key points within the message; place the key points of the message at either the beginning or the end; or make sure the message's key points are more emotionally arousing than its other content? And does your message use the previous three principles overall to make it more memorable relative to other messages?

In addition, make sure your message uses at least one of the following techniques to enhance its persuasiveness:

- **Autopilot** Does your message contain: scarcity signals to make the desired behaviour more urgent; perceived social proof to make the desired behaviour seem more popular; cues of authority to make the desired behaviour seem more acceptable; reciprocity to encourage people to do the desired behaviour in return for a gift; liking to make the message and its target behaviour more accepted among recipients; or commitment and consistency to make recipients bind themselves to the desired behaviour.

- **Priming** Does your message use appropriate stimuli to plant ideas in recipients' heads in order to influence their behaviour – such as superhero imagery to encourage prosocial actions?

13 PROMOTIONS

The Friday following Thanksgiving is known as 'Black Friday' in the US; it is the day when stores open their doors earlier and entice customers in with pre-Christmas sales. In 2008, a crowd of 2,000 eager shoppers burst through the doors of a Long Island Wal-Mart so that they could get into the store early and snap up the bargains before the rest of the throng; in their stampede, one Wal-Mart employee was knocked to the floor and trampled to death.[1]

Black Friday appears to generally be an orgy of greed-driven mayhem; since 2006, there have been 89 injuries attributable to the event, there have been 41 reports of customers using pepper spray on one another, and in 2012 two people were shot.[2]

Consumers are *not* rational – contrary to the traditional approach.

Rather than trying to inform or persuade, the goal for successful advertising is typically *memory*[3] – that is, advertising essentially makes a brand *self-relevant* so that it is more likely to catch a consumer's attention.

An excellent illustration of this comes from the Dasani experiment mentioned previously:[4] when participants weren't exposed to any pictures subtly containing the Dasani brand, 17% chose the brand to drink; after exposure to twelve such pictures, the proportion rose to 40%. Ultimately, advertisements put a brand inside consumers' heads in order to influence choice.

The formula for effective adverts

Break through	+ Get absorbed	+ Stay absorbed
Use emotion, surprise, sex, food or faces to make sure your advert gets the attention of busy consumers	Make sure your ad, or series of ads, tells a story; alternatively, pique the curiosity of viewers	Use a reach strategy: repetition is key. Use consistent elements in the adverts to make them sticky

The story is very similar for other promotions beyond advertising, as well.

Approximately 50% of all fast-moving consumer goods in the UK are bought on price promotion, with a 26% average discount.[5] This is an awful lot of money to brands, and the problem is they just don't work. While discounts may produce a *short-term* sales increase, in the long-run they are ineffectual for a range of reasons, including the brand becoming devalued, consumers refusing to pay a higher price, consumers stock-piling when prices are low, and so on.[6]

The issue here is ostensibly that brands are using promotions as a tool to rationally influence consumer choice. However, research suggests that shoppers do not actually use discounts in a rational way: in-store research has shown that less than 15% of shoppers are able to remember the prices of goods they had just recently placed in their basket, for example.[7]

Instead, promotional materials ought to increase *physical availability*[7] – that is, they should make a brand easy to see or find. In this sense, the most important function for promotions is to draw attention to a brand. As an illustration, a large-scale study of panel data found that just being on promotion, irrespective of the size of the discount, increases sales:[8] perhaps promotions have their sales effects simply because they draw attention to products. In-store signage can result in a 142% sales increase.[9]

In this vein, the effectiveness of price promotions can be greatly enhanced simply by grabbing attention.

What's more, promotions can also be made more effective through an intelligent use of heuristics. These can be used to nudge behaviour – for example, people will buy more ice-cream sandwiches if a sign simply saying, 'Buy 18 for your freezer', is added to the promotion.[10]

The formula for effective promotions

Get product seen	+ Get product bought
Use any of the following techniques to get people to see the product: colour contrast; movement; sound; emotion; faces; food; sex; surprise; personalisation	Use heuristics to: increase the perceived benefits of buying (e.g. scarcity to increase its value); and reduce the perceived costs (i.e. price psychology)

On the whole, consumers are cognitive misers who spend very little time thinking or caring about brands; the most important thing for a brand is to get inside people's heads and to be easy to buy. The principles outlined in this book for getting people hooked can be applied to promotions as follows.

Invite attention

- **Be creative or emotional** to succeed. Rational arguments are an added bonus: they can be nice, but they are by no means necessary. Likewise, sex sells; it's a cliché but it's absolutely true. Plus, cute animals and babies are a sure-fire winner, as are threatening things like spiders and snakes.

- **Forget about attitudes** – don't worry whether people like your advert (most of them will not care enough) – what's more important is that they remember it. Is it more important to be liked or bought?

- **Use images** where possible, particularly moving ones. Similarly, noises are good for getting attention, particularly loud ones.

- **Take advantage of new technology** to make adverts as attention-grabbing and engaging as possible – whether this is using 'big data' to personalise banner ads, using TV screen billboards instead of traditional posters, or even using technology like facial coding to make adverts which respond to people's smiles.

- **Personalise** adverts wherever possible; customisation is not entirely feasible yet for mass communications, so a better route may be to use commonly familiar stimuli like celebrities or holiday festivals.

- **Get products seen** in-store using promotional materials – attention should be the priority, not communicating a discount. Often we like what we see more than we see what we like.

- **Use the principles** of emotion, primality, personalisation and surprise to make in-store promotional materials as attention-grabbing as possible. For example, make signage an unusual colour, or slap a picture of a kitten on it.

- **Distinctive assets** (outlined below) are vital for advertising – they make it easier for consumers to notice, find and remember brands, and, if done right, they can also be very good at getting attention.

DISTINCTIVE ASSETS

There is a branding principle which can help to bring all of these elements together and enhance the efficacy of advertising. 'Distinctive assets' are perceptual elements unique to a brand like a logo, colour, font, jingle, celebrity, mascot, and so on; they are vital to brand growth.[11]

One example in particular comes from the Felix brand of cat food in the UK.[12] In 1998, Felix accounted for just 5% of the market in single-serve wet cat food pouches; the market leader, Whiskas, had actually pioneered the product. However, over the next five years, Felix actually came to overtake Whiskas as the market leader, all while consistently spending less than half the amount that Whiskas was spending on advertising.

▶

Source: © Newscast-online Limited/Alamy Stock Photo

Share of single serve cat food

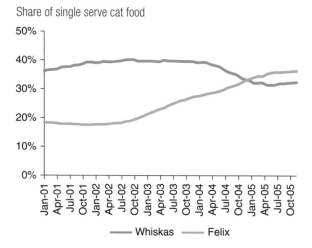

While Whiskas tried a variety of different (and, importantly, inconsistent) advertising campaigns over the years, Felix used the same series of ads with different permutations, enjoying the benefits of both repeated exposure and novelty.

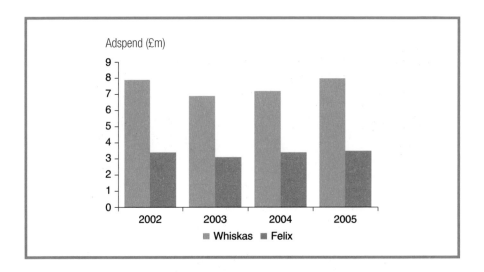

Ignite thinking

- **Build narrative** into advertisements: those which use stories are more effective than those without.

- **Adverts should be simple** – as simple as possible in fact, as research has shown script complexity is negatively related to effectiveness. Likewise, the shorter the sweeter when it comes to slogans and ad copy.

- **Prioritise images over words**, for both advertisements and promotions.

- **Use curiosity and mystery** in adverts to pique your audience's interest – give your audience puzzles or riddles to solve. Metaphors are particularly useful.

- **Fluency is paramount** in promotions – make the product as easy to find and buy as possible (i.e. utilise physical availability to the maximum).

Incite action

- **Use a reach strategy** for advertising, if it is to work: reach as many people as possible as many times as possible.

- **Be the emotional peak** of the context in which the advert sits – for example, do not advertise during highly arousing sex or violence content.

- **Do not crowd out your message** in your advert by over-the-top emotion which may be remembered instead.

- **Credibility is important** for the persuasiveness of adverts: using celebrities, personal accounts, and statistics can all act as credibility-enhancing heuristics.

- **Prime** The general goal of advertising should be priming – that is, making a brand mentally salient in order to influence choice.

- **Don't worry if an advert is not consciously remembered**: it does not need to be explicitly recalled in order have an effect on behaviour (implicit memory is important, too).

- **Price psychology heuristics** are vital for promotions: they are a cost-effective and powerful way to make discounts less expensive for a brand. Some examples are given in the table below.

Key price psychology principles

Principle	Explanation
Yellow background[13]	A price/discount will be perceived as better value if written on a yellow background, since yellow is associated with discounts.
Reference price[14]	A reference price (e.g. 'Was £2, now £1') makes the sale price appear to be better value by comparison.
Font size[15]	A sale price in a smaller font than the reference price causes the buyer to perceive the sale price as, literally, smaller.
Phonemes[16]	Prices with phonemes associated with smallness (e.g. 'teeny tiny') are seen as smaller – which may be why 99 works well.
Product descriptors[17]	Accompanying the price with, say, 'Low Maintenance' (versus 'High Reliability') results in the price being seen as lower.
Charm prices[18]	Certain price endings, especially 99, are associated with value; raising a price to a 99 end can actually increase sales.
Precise prices[19]	Large numbers are usually rounded up, so prices with 00s are perceived as high, and precise prices (e.g. £1.26) as low.
Bundling[20]	Bundling products/prices together increases product evaluations and sales, as discounts are inferred.
Drip pricing[21]	'Dripping' the full price through stages is effective because consumers commit to the product at the first, cheaper price.
Product options[22]	Consumers pay more options when starting with 'the full Monty' and then removing features, due to being loss averse.
Price length[23]	The more digits a number has, the larger it is seen to be; so dropping the pennies, or having them small (e.g. £1.26) is best.
Price obfuscation[24]	Prices are associated with a painful loss, so hiding the fact a price is a price (e.g. by losing the £) can be beneficial.
Time limit[25]	Making a promotion time-limited or saying 'While Supplies Last' increases sales efficacy.

14 THE PSYCH OF LIKE

Jean Twenge has discovered something that may not be a surprise to most of us: we are becoming more narcissistic.[1] For example, one of the studies found that the narcissism score for recent survey respondents was 30% higher than those in the 1980s.[2] Another experiment gives a clue as to why this might be: participants completed a standard measure of narcissism after either editing their MySpace profile or using Google Maps, and, as you may have guessed, the former group scored higher on narcissism.[3]

The fact is that social media (and the internet) is becoming such a huge part of our lives that it is changing who we are: in fact, it is literally rewiring our brains.[4] An estimated 500 million Tweets are sent every day,[5] by consumers who spend almost a third of each full day staring at screens.[6]

While this is ostensibly a fantastic opportunity when it comes to getting messages seen, it is important to realise that people are just as much cognitive misers online as they are offline: one study determined that the average online user's attention span is just eight seconds.[7] It is for this reason that many studies have demonstrated the efficacy of the principles outlined so far in this book for making online messages work.

The authors of one fantastic paper used a computer program to analyse three months of articles on *The New York Times*' website: each article underwent sentiment analysis, in which the article's words were analysed for certain

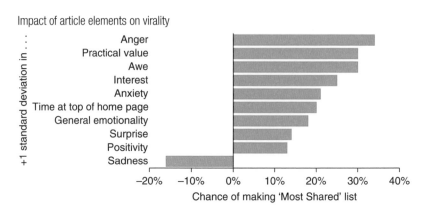

Impact of article elements on virality

themes.[8] The researchers also had data on whether or not the article appeared on the site's 'Most emailed' list (i.e. was viral). As can be seen in the chart above, a standard deviation increase in the emotionality of an article made it 18% more likely to be viral.

An analysis of Buzzfeed article headlines provides further evidence for the power of these principles to get online content read.[9] A software engineer in San Francisco analysed Buzzfeed headlines by splitting them into three-word phrases and then recording the number of Facebook shares for each; as can be seen in the chart below, certain phrases are more popular than others.

Impact of Buzzfeed headline on Facebook shares

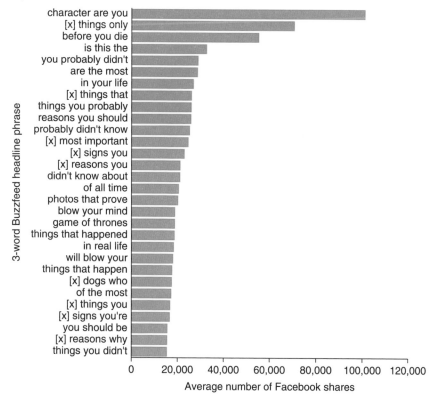

Source: Adapted from boingboing.net

Personalisation emerged as a dominant theme, with many of the most popular articles telling readers something about themselves; curiosity was also a major factor, with the classic link bait phrase '. . . you probably didn't know' appearing to be popular.

PSYCH OF LIKE CASE STUDY

By taking fluent phrases like #wonderfilled, repeating them on a regular basis, and incorporating them into fun, emotional and engaging activities around the same time as the 2014 Winter Olympics in Canada, Oreo was able to win a 2.5% increase in its penetration in the market and a 16.3% increase in market share.[10]

In the end, online content ostensibly follows the same rules of effectiveness as other messages, except that memory is perhaps of less importance since online content is typically more urgent. Other than that, online content needs to get attention and incite an action; the formula for an affective online message is presented below.

The formula for effective online content

Be simple	+	Excite	+	Inspire action
Use fluency (numbered lists are especially effective), be short and simple, and send the message out at the time of highest exposure.		Use a phrase which: uses a high-arousal emotion; is surprising or unexpected; presents brand new information. Alternatively, include an emoticon.		Include a phrase which uses either curiosity to encourage people to click through, or heuristics to encourage them to act.

On the whole, people are cognitive misers online too – they react to websites in just a twentieth of a second, for example. If anything, attention spans may be even more fractured on the internet. Practical applications for 'the psych of like' are as follows.

INVITE ATTENTION

- **Emotion is the most important** factor in social updates and online content like articles and videos according to research: specifically, it should be highly arousing, and negative emotions tend to do better than bad ones.
- **Know what people want** online and use it to entice them. As a great illustration, a strong predictor of success of Kickstarter campaigns was found by one study to be the use of the word 'cats' in the pitch![11]

- **Emoticons** can capture attention in a similar fashion to faces. Research shows that the brain responds to emoticons in much the same way as faces,[12] and that Tweets are more likely to be shared if they contain emoticons.[13]

- **Faces** alone are powerful online as well as offline; have a clear facial picture in your profile picture or avatar, for example, to get people's attention (and to endear them to you).

- **Personalisation** is very easy to do online and it is extremely effective: include people's names, locations, or other personal information in online content when possible – and make the most of new 'big data' opportunities to understand what makes your audience tick.

- **Make content self-relevant** as well; personal discovery content and quizzes (e.g. 'What kind of potato are you?') are extremely popular.

IGNITE THINKING

- **Use questions** to engage potential readers through the principle of curiosity. One piece of research discovered that Tweets containing question marks are more likely to be retweeted.[14]

- **Make content surprising** – bizarre, unintuitive or new information will make readers curious and encourage them to turn that link from blue to purple. There is a lot of 'noise' online and people are very thirsty for anything new or engaging.

- **Keep things short and simple**, and don't overload the message with content. What is the one key thing you want it to communicate? While a large study showed that more useful information, such as hashtags or links) increases the virality of a Tweet, it also showed that too much information is damaging; the optimum length is 100–120 characters.[15]

- **Post content at the optimum time** to maximise its digital 'physical availability': submit it at the highest-traffic days and times for your audience (typically weekends, and lunch and evenings in the week). Facebook and Twitter engagement rates are 32% and 17% higher, respectively, at the weekend; and during the week, Twitter engagement is highest around 12 pm and 6 pm.[15]

- **Attach images** to your posts, as they are always effective at both catching attention and communicating a message.

- **Use infographics** (or at least charts and diagrams) wherever possible – they are very good at communicating information, and people not only love to read them, but share them as well.

- **Narrative** itself is of limited use in the world of the 140-character Tweet; however, the individual use of empathy, archetypes and meaning-making can all make online messages more impactful.

- **Build stories in the long term** through your content: rather than disparate series of posts, link things together with meaning, mystery and dramatic tension so that your audience is kept eagerly waiting for the next update.

INCITE ACTION

- **Post each message multiple times**: reminder posts have been shown to increase the effectiveness of online campaigns. In fact, one of the strongest predictors of a Kickstarter campaign's success is how many reminder emails are sent out.[16]

- **Be the emotional peak** in your audience's newsfeed. Your post is likely to get ignored and forgotten if it's posted at the same time a celebrity scandal breaks.

- **Heuristics** will make social content more behaviourally persuasive. To illustrate, Kickstarter campaigns can be made more likely to be successful by using heuristics like scarcity (e.g. writing phrases like, 'You are being given the chance to . . .').[11]

- **Give readers something for free** in order to encourage reciprocity – a low-cost giveaway like a free download, or even a joke, weather forecast or interesting fact, will do the trick.

- **Don't exploit your audience** by spamming them with messages or constantly asking for help. On the Reddit forum 'Random Acts of Pizza', where people ask strangers to buy them a pizza delivery for free, a strong predictor of success is reciprocity – paying back the favour.[17]

- **Be trustworthy and credible** (i.e. use the authority heuristic) when communicating online as trust is low and scepticism is high: use the correct signals to do this. On 'Random Acts of Pizza', the number of 'karma' points a user has when asking for pizza is a strong predictor of success as well.[17]

- Engage recipients on a first-name basis if possible, in order to encourage liking. Building emotional relationships with recipients is similarly effective for influencing behaviour – for example, build a conversation about the products they have bought from you in the past (e.g. 'Hi John, I hope you're enjoying the toaster you bought in January!').

- Show or imply that many others are reading your posts: the inferred social proof will increase engagement. The number of retweets a post has is a significant influence on whether or not a person will read it,[18] and that the time spent reading a news article is positively predicted by the average five-star rating it has been given.[19]

EXERCISE

An effective Tweet

Rewrite the following three Tweets using the formula outlined above:

1 Prostate cancer Tweet

Please click here to donate to the prostate cancer fund and help the 14% of men who will be diagnosed #canceruk.

How would you write part of a new and improved Tweet that would:

> be simple;
> excite;
> inspire action.

Now put it all together.

2 Cinema press release Tweet

Click here to have a look at what our 3D SCREENS will be able to do next year!

How would you write part of a new and improved Tweet that would:

> be simple;
> excite;
> inspire action.

Now put it all together.

3 Fast-food menu Tweet

NEW Chicken fillet – made of all natural ingredients.

How would you write part of a new and improved Tweet that would:

be simple;
excite;
inspire action.

Now put it all together.

15 DIRECT MAIL

A January 2014 *Daily Mail* article reported on an American cat who hated junk mail – every time the postman tried to deliver some, he'd get such a ferocious mauling that he once lost a glove.[1]

Well, actually the cat attacked *anything* that came through the letterbox – and it was probably acting out its catty instincts rather than expressing a distaste for the occasional unwanted SkyMall brochure. However, the spin given to the story highlights a salient point: we love to hate direct mail.

In fact, a 2004 BBC documentary, *Brassed-Off Britain,* conducted a poll and found that junk mail was deemed the number one most irritating thing in the country – supported by a survey finding that two-thirds of Brits objected to direct mail and just under a third found it intrusive.[2] Given the choice, the majority of people (77%) will opt-out of receiving direct mail from companies they don't deal with.[3]

However, here's the thing: direct mail is actually very effective. People might hate it, but – just like the adverts by HeadOn and Go Compare – it still works.

One survey of marketers found it to be the channel with the highest return on investment for customer acquisition.[4] Researchers at the University of Sydney even managed to put a figure on it:[5] after observing three weeks of baseline sales in a major Australian retailer, a leaflet advertising current promotions was posted to consumers living in the local area of each store. This had a significant effect on sales for all product categories tested in the leaflet, with average units sold per week increasing by figures ranging from 68% for liquid detergent to a massive 1,167% for sandwich toasters.

So, direct marketing is a powerful tool for any company – how can you make it work for you?

Using the two most widespread forms of direct marketing in the UK – post and email[6] – this chapter will explain how the previous psychological principles apply to increasing their effectiveness. Specifically, there are three steps.

Again, the first thing any letter or email needs to do is get *noticed*. In 2014, British consumers received approximately 3.2 billion unaddressed pieces of junk mail.[7] If each piece was as thick as regular A4 paper, the stack would be

18 times as high as Mount Everest – and that excludes direct mail *addressed* to the recipient. In digital terms, over 100 billion spam emails are sent every day worldwide.[8] With our limited attention spans, a lot of this will simply be ignored. The Direct Marketing Association reported that 20% and 54% of people open, respectively, emails and letters straight away whoever they may be from, meaning a good many people are more selective.[9]

Once a piece of direct mail is noticed, the next step is to be *opened* and read. To illustrate, if an email appears to be marketing something, 17% of people will delete it without reading, and 9% will do so for letters.[9] Therefore it is important that the message not only get attention but also be designed in such a way as to actually hook audiences.

Finally, the third step is of course to get recipients to *act* on the message they have read, using simplicity and intelligent 'nudges'.

The formula for effective direct mail

Get seen	+	Get opened	+	Inspire action
Use personalisation and/or surprise at the point of contact with the recipient; use multiple exposures to make the message salient.		Use authority, curiosity and/or narrative to encourage recipients to actually read the message.		Once the message has been opened, use heuristics to make the letter or email effective at influencing behaviour.

On the whole, despite there being a lot of it, and consumer perceptions generally being unfavourable, direct mail is relatively effective; it can be made more so using psychological principles.

INVITING ATTENTION

- **Personalise** the message at the point of contact (e.g. on the front of the envelope or in the subject line) to catch your recipient's attention. Researchers at the Bowman Gray School of Medicine conducted an experiment in which 1,000 households were posted information about cervical cancer and given the chance to enter a prize draw by returning a postage-paid postcard:[10] envelopes which included the recipient's name saw a response rate of 21%, compared to 13% for those which read 'resident'.

- **Use memory/priming to make the message more self-relevant**, so that it gets noticed. In other words, prime the recipient to recognise the message by making it front-of-mind. A review of almost 300 studies found that the likelihood of a survey being completed was increased by 54% through contacting participants before sending them the mail.[11]

- **Use multiple, different touchpoints** In essence, the more points of contact the better; for example, send an email, a text message *and* a letter, if it is feasible.

- **Surprise** is also a good means to catch attention at this point – providing it is cost-effective, make the envelope (or, if possible, email) different so that the recipient will hold off from throwing it away just to find out what it is. Initiatives that have increased response rates include writing the address in green ink,[12] putting a sticker on the envelope,[13] and using a larger-than-normal envelope.[14]

- **Use unusual materials** as well. The Royal Mail used biometric and neurometric methods and found that more interesting mail – e.g., cut into an unusual shape, incorporating holograms, or made of heavyweight card – were better at getting attention and resulted in more favourable perceptions and behaviours.[15]

- **However, avoid ostentatiousness with charity appeals**: such envelopes can backfire because they imply that the charity is wasting money they could be spending on their cause.[16]

EXAMPLES OF INVITING ATTENTION FOR DIRECT MAIL

Fiskar scissors demonstrated the power of using a surprising piece of direct mail to grab recipients' attention and engage them in the message.[17] Recipients received an intricate silhouette in place of a letter; the company enjoyed a 53% response rate and a 19% increase in order volumes compared to the previous month.

Next, the British-American cruise line Carnival showed how personalisation could increase direct mail effectiveness by grabbing attention, engaging recipients, and causing recipients to like what they had received.[18] Recipients received a letter which was totally customised to their own holiday-related interests – information the brand had gathered previously. For example, some recipients' letters spoke to the fact that their children love cruises, while others focused on gaming like blackjack and slots. Compared to the non-personalised campaign in the previous year, this initiative had an 80% higher response rate and generated 37% more bookings.

IGNITE THINKING

- **Use materials which encourage touching**, when it comes to physical direct mail, so that people will pick up the message. Once people touch something, they feel a greater sense of ownership, meaning the recipient may be less likely to bin, and more likely to open, the letter.

- **Make the message tangible** One paper sent a request for survey participation to 500 British university staff, finding that 72% responded to the posted surveys, and 34% to emails.[19]

- **Send letters by recorded delivery** as a study found that doing so made posted questionnaires almost twice as likely to be filled in.[11] Do anything, like this, which makes the message more noticeable or mentally salient.

- **Send messages at the best time and day** There is, for instance, evidence that response rates to posted direct mail are highest just before or just after the weekend,[20] while email open and click rates are highest on weekends and, during weekdays, highest during the morning.[21] Physical direct mail is better than digital direct mail; although the materials involved suggest the latter may be more cost-effective.

- **Use curiosity**, such as a blank email subject line, which creates a mystery which can only be solved by opening it and reading the letter. An in-field study found that including a teaser in the form of a question on the envelope made direct mail significantly more effective.[14]

- **Build a story** over the course of the messages: recipients will open them to find out how the narrative arc is progressing. A study found that charitable donations were increased by consistently telling a story showing recipients how their donations are making a difference.[22]

- **Be simple** Make the message as short as possible, and include pictures over text where feasible, in order to make things easy for recipients. The likelihood of a response has been shown to increase by 86% when a shorter questionnaire is used and by 121% when a stamped return envelope is included;[11] and, a survey of email marketing experts found that direct mail emails were thought to be more effective when they included fewer scroll-downs (i.e. less content) and more images.[23]

INCITE ACTION

- **Signal authority** at the point of contact in order to encourage recipients to trust, and therefore open, the message. A review found that surveys from official institutions like universities had a 31% higher chance of a response than those from commercial organisations, and surveys had a 12% higher chance of response when sent via first class.[11]

- **Use authority to motivate action**, as well as to motivate opening the message. People are more likely to complete a survey, for example, if it is accompanied by a cover letter signed by an appropriate expert.[24]

- **Be personable** with the recipient and make it clear who the message is coming from, or else their trust is likely to be low. Sending an email from an impersonal address (e.g. surveys@gold.ac.uk) received a lower response rate than from a personal address (e.g. p.fagan@gold.ac.uk).[25]

- **Make sure the recipients like the sender**, inasmuch as this is possible. One study found that direct mail advertisements were much more effective if they included a picture of an attractive woman.[26]

- **Include a small, free gift** to encourage action via reciprocity – again, even an interesting fact will do.

- **Be creative with using heuristics**: there are endless possibilities. To give just one example, 'future discounting' is where people value money less in the future than they do in the present[27] – asking donors to increase their donations 'two months from now' was shown to increase donations by 32% compared to 'today', in one experiment.[28]

EXERCISE

Creating effective direct mail

You are creating a piece of direct mail – a letter to send to all of the customers of your small locksmith business. Currently, you send people a letter typed on A4 and posted to recipients inside a standard brown envelope with the recipient's name typed on the front. How might you change each of the following to make it more effective? Assume money is no object.

What would you do to the shape and format of the envelope?
What would you write on the front of the envelope?
What one single sentence might you add to the letter?

16 IN THE OFFICE

British workers spend an average of 42.7 hours a week at work.[1] Excluding weekends and holidays (although many of us spend most of those working as well), that means we spend a *third* of our adult lives working – that's over half of our *waking* adult lives.

It's little wonder, then, that the workplace has a significant, causal impact on our happiness[2] and wellbeing;[3] clearly there is a lot of value to doing well in the workplace.

Unsurprisingly, psychological factors have a significant effect on workplace success. To give just one example as an illustration, one study of public-company CEOs found that a 22.1 Hz decrease in voice pitch was associated with an increase in the size of the firm managed to the tune of $440 million, and a related $187,000 increase in pay.[4]

Indeed, the first part of effective messages in the workplace involves interpersonal influence. Whether it's an interview, presentation or pitch, the evidence suggests you will be much more successful if you exercise social influence. As American investment banker Ziad K. Abdelnour once said, 'Seek respect, not attention. It lasts longer.'[5]

Having said that, the second key point for effective workplace communication is to be engaging – that is, to get your audience to pay attention to what you're saying, and process it cognitively. As in all message contexts, businesspeople have limited attention spans: it is estimated that people begin to zone out of presentations after 10–15 minutes, at the most.[6]

The third point is that heuristics and priming can be used to influence decisions in your favour during workplace communications. Experts in interpersonal influence excel in the workplace.

The formula for effective workplace communication

Be liked +	Engage +	'Nudge'
Use your clothing, body language, speech and actions to be a charismatic speaker: use authority and liking extensively.	Spice up your content with the principles outlined in this book – including narrative, curiosity and surprise.	Get the upper hand in business meetings and pitches by incorporating heuristics and priming.

On the whole, succeeding at work is vital for our happiness and wellbeing – but do we put enough thought into it? Psychology can help pitches, presentations and meetings go more smoothly.

INVITE ATTENTION

- **Use images and animations** in your slides to get attention – sounds are useful as well, but don't overdo it as they can be distracting. Research has shown they enhance comprehension.[7] Always incorporate videos into presentations where feasible – at any rate, avoid reams of dull, monotonous text or speech.

- **Be creative in using contrast** to get attention – such as punctuating important points with a loud clap.

- **Incorporate emotional stimuli** – and include images and words – that will get your audience's attention; examples might be pictures of babies, pictures of faces, swear words, and so on.

- **Have a sense of humour** when meeting people or giving presentations – humour is very good at activating the amygdala (i.e. engaging people emotionally).[8]

- **Don't be afraid of the unusual** Including emotional images, telling jokes, clapping, and so on, will all captivate your audience, but you may be concerned about how people will perceive you. Well, remember that attitudes are far less important than behaviours. Do you want the client to buy what you're selling, or to like you?

- **Be personally distinctive** – you don't have to wear a polka-dotted bow tie everywhere, but unique, noticeable earrings or cufflinks will earn you attention personally in your career without being crass.

IGNITE THINKING

- **Present interesting and new content** Make sure your audience has not heard everything before – if that is unavoidable, find a way to present it in a new light.

- **Don't be dry** In other words, don't present statistics and bullet points one after another – remember that we are dominated by our 'monkey brain'. Keep things light and fun.

- Tell stories: presentations are more effective when the information is presented as a narrative.[9]
- Use narrative case studies and examples as well as statistics in order to make the information more persuasive and memorable.[10]
- Ask questions of your audience – both rhetorical and actual – to get them thinking. Research shows this enhances presentations' effectiveness.[11]
- Use mystery to pique the curiosity of your audience – make facts a secret to be revealed over time, rather than just giving them away up-front.
- Incorporate puzzles and exercises into your presentation to make them interesting, too. When the audience has a problem to solve, they better remember the content.[12]
- Hold meetings face-to-face rather than digitally or over the phone – or, at least, use video conferencing. This will make the communication more concrete and tangible, and therefore more persuasive.

INCITE ACTION

- Repeat key points throughout the presentation to make them memorable; also make sure to repeat them at the beginning and the end of the presentation.
- Be likeable in order to be persuasive. One study videotaped a clip of a manager – who was actually an actor – interacting with employees, and participants rated how competent he was;[13] when the manager was seen displaying liking signals (such as asking, 'How are you doing?') he was rated as significantly more competent.
- Use similarity as a route to liking. As an example, Americans were asked to listen to an audio clip of a candidate applying for a job and rate how likely they would be to give the candidate the role; however, the applicant's accent varied.[14] These American participants were much more favourable towards the American-accented candidate.
- Use body language to be liked – for example, mirror people's stances, expressions and gestures (known as 'mimicking'),[15] physically touching them,[16] and smiling at them.[17]
- Be as attractive as you can! Attractive job candidates are more likely to be hired,[18] while obese candidates fare poorly in job interviews.[19]

- **Disclose personal information** by, for example, telling a personal story about yourself to illustrate a point. A large meta-analysis found a clear link between self-disclosure and liking, such that people who told stories about their own lives were liked more.[20]

- **Don't be *too* likable** as authority is also a powerful influencer and it is often the antitheses of liking. Personality researchers have shown that nice guys really do finish last: among men, being agreeable – that is, warm, friendly and trusting – is linked to a significantly lower salary.[21] Smiling and nodding too much are harmful for workplace authority and persuasion.[22]

- **Use clothes to communicate authority**. One study found that job applicants, both male and female, who wore masculine clothing were seen as more competent, and were more likely to be hired;[23] and studies have shown for many years that people who wear glasses are rated as more intelligent, honest, hard-working and reliable.[24]

- **Maintain good eye contact** to signal authority as well. Interviewees who avert their gaze are rated by interviewers as less credible, and are less likely to be hired.[25] However, total, unrelenting gaze can have the opposite effect[26] – don't overdo it!

- **A firm handshake** is good – it has been positively linked to an interviewer's likelihood of recommending someone for the role.[27]

- **Speak with authority**; speaking faster and with fewer pauses, a constant volume, a lower pitch and more variability in pitch is positively linked to better workplace outcomes.[28]

- **Be creative with heuristics** to 'nudge' your attendees, clients or colleagues in the direction you desire. To give an example, it is possible to influence the negotiating behaviours of a client during a pitch, or an employer during a salary review – that is, if you start the negotiating by suggesting a very high (even ludicrously high) sum, you will end up getting more than if you did otherwise.[29]

- **Be creative with priming** to likewise influence the behaviour and decisions of your peers. For instance, negotiators will be more cooperative and give greater concessions if you call them a partner rather than an opponent;[30] and they will be more likely to accept unfair offers if they are primed with sad stimuli like a depressing video clip;[31] but if you mention money too often, they could become more individualistic and unempathetic.[32]

YOUR PRESENTATION CHECKLIST

You are putting together a presentation for an important prospective client. Make sure you have each of the following elements:

- **Narrative i** Does your presentation tell a story from start to finish?
- **Narrative ii** Does your presentation include small stories as illustrative case studies? Stories from your own personal life are better.
- **Questions** Do you ask interactive questions of your audience through the presentation?
- **Exercises** As well as the questions, do you have engaging puzzles or exercises throughout the presentation to keep people engaged?
- **Mystery** Do you tease the audience at some point by alluding to some interesting information but keeping it secret until later?
- **Images** Is your presentation more image than text?
- **Simplicity** Is your presentation as short, simple and concrete as possible? Make sure not to bore people with stats and bullet points, and make sure any points you make could be easily understood by a child.
- **Contrast** Do you use movement and/or sound in your presentation? Videos are particularly good.
- **Interest** Does your presentation contain new, interesting and exciting content – if not the whole way through, at least in select places?
- **Liking** Are you relaxed and charismatic before presenting, making sure to smile and make eye contact?
- **Authority** Have you dressed smartly, and practiced your slow, deliberate body language and speech? Rehearsing and knowing what you are going to say is absolutely key.

A power booster

Before you enter a meeting or go on stage to present, improve your perceived authority by simply spending a couple of minutes in a 'power stance' – for example, lean back in a chair with your feet on the desk and your hands folded behind your head. A 'power stance' involves taking up lots of space and having open arms and legs.

▶

Researchers from Colombia University and Harvard recently carried out a study in which participants used a 'power stance' for two minutes before completing a barrage of psychological and behavioural tests of dominance.[33] Compared to people who sat or stood in stances associated with low status, the participants were, by all measures, higher in power. For instance, the 'power stance' resulted in higher feelings of power, higher risk-taking and higher levels of testosterone.

It's a case, then, of 'fake it 'til you make it'. Stand in a confidence pose for two minutes before your meeting or presentation, and you will likely present more authoritatively and confidently.

17 TEST, TEST, TEST

'Life, uh, finds a way.'

So said Jeff Goldblum's sexy mathematician (!) character Ian Malcolm in *Jurassic Park*. There is a fantastic scene where Goldblum's character explains chaos theory to the trip's paleobotanist using water from a plastic cup: every time a drop falls on her hand, it rolls down a different route due to tiny, unpredictable variations in the environment. A major theme in *Jurassic Park* is how life is chaotic, unpredictable and uncontrollable.

The next time Goldblum's plastic cup of water is seen, it vibrates ominously to announce the arrival of a Tyrannosaurus Rex. Despite the best efforts of the park's owner, the beast could not be contained, due to a confluence of unpredictable forces like the park's security measures being shut down by a greedy employee with thieving intentions.

Outside the world of blockbuster entertainment, the infamous Murphy's Law – 'Anything that can go wrong, will go wrong' – was allegedly coined by aerospace engineer Edward Murphy in response to finding inconsistent or unusual results across scientific tests, due to factors which were hard to control.[1]

The point is that the world is a chaotic and unpredictable place. What we expect to work, or what has worked elsewhere, might not work for us in our own specific context.

This has important implications for designing sticky messages.

I was once told about a consultancy who advised a big British brand on their direct mail – specifically, how to change a promotional letter to make it more effective. The brand's existing letter was put through a psychological meat grinder: it was rearranged and updated to include emotion, fluency and heuristics, among other things. In theory, it was perfect.

In practice, it resulted in the worst response rate the company had ever seen.

Everything discussed in this book is based on science, and, to be blunt, is vastly more effective than the use of hunches and assumptions generally involved with designing messages. However, it is important to test these principles for yourself within your own, personal context.

So how should you do this?

The ideal would be to measure a behaviour. Whatever your message, the ultimate goal will almost always be to affect some kind of action – whether it's visiting a website, buying a product or eating more fruit and vegetables.

This should be done through a randomised control trial, where – to put it simply – one group of participants is a control group, and another group of participants, matched on important variables like demographics – is the experimental group. For example, as a test of curiosity, the control group might be sent a Tweet saying, 'Our website will make you smile,' while the experimental group receives, 'Will our website make you smile?'

There are certain instances where measuring the outcome behaviour is very simple: split-testing can be easily carried out in the digital world, where, for example, recipients randomly receive one of two types of email and you simply see which type results in the most clicks. Online services like Mailchimp and Optimizely make this extremely easy.

However, sometimes measuring the outcome behaviour is not always feasible or desirable. You may, for example, want to test the effectiveness of a new leaflet, advert or package *before* spending money producing it and taking a risk releasing it into the world. Alternatively, you may want to understand *why* exactly one message is more effective than another.

In these instances, it's tempting to just ask people. For instance, if you want to know if people would buy your product after seeing your pitch, why not show the pitch to a test group and ask them, 'Would this make you buy the product?'

Unfortunately, traditional survey methodologies are extremely flawed.

Imagine, for example, that you work as a digital strategy manager at Blacks, the outdoor clothing and supplies retailer. You are creating a new website and you want to know what influences people's choices of tent purchases online. How would you measure this?

One study did indeed set up a mock online site where people were shown a range of different tents varying in price, colour, size, and so on.[2] After participants had chosen their favourite one, they were asked why they picked it over the others. Attributes like weatherproofing and insect repelling were deemed most important – but the most important factor was presentation order, with the first-presented tent being picked 2.5 times more than any other.

The major problem with explicitly asking people for their responses is that they have little to no awareness of the subconscious drivers of their behaviour; they cannot report on why they behaved a certain way, or how they would respond to a message, because they simply do not know.

Remember: 'The human brain is like a monkey brain with a cortical "press secretary" who is glib at concocting explanations for behaviour, and who privileges deliberative explanations over cruder ones.'[3]

What's more, survey methodologies are subject to a range of cognitive biases which invalidate people's answers – like the fact that people will rate Tony Blair as more honest if asked to do so on a –5 to +5 scale than a 0 to 11 scale,[4] or that 30% of respondents in one study gave their opinion on The Agricultural Trades Act of 1978, which, actually, didn't even exist.[5]

Other explicit methodologies can be equally unreliable, often because people feel pressured to respond a certain way;[6] New Coke tested well in focus groups.[7]

So explicitly asking people is not always a fantastic method for testing. Alternatively, research has shown that implicit – that is, indirect or non-conscious – methodologies are often better at predicting behaviour.[8] A small overview of these methodologies follows.

For example, 'implicit testing' is the use of reaction times to measure non-conscious associations in memory. The method was originally, and most famously, used to measure non-conscious racial prejudice among participants.[9] For example, if they hesitated to press a button to group good words like 'pleasant' into the category 'Black Faces/Good Words', but did not hesitate to group bad words like 'unpleasant' into 'Black Faces/Bad Words' then the association between black people and the idea of 'bad' was strong in their minds.

Implicit testing can be used to measure people's cognitive reactions to messages. For example, are they quicker to associate 'sugar' with 'bad' after an anti-sugar message? Alternatively, it could be used to measure how memorable a message is by, for instance, measuring reaction times for recognising elements of the message a week after seeing it.

There are, in theory, almost unlimited uses for implicit testing, which is one of its advantages. Additionally, it is very cheap and easy to carry out, with the price being comparable to surveys and the test being administrable online; despite its ease of use, implicit testing is also extremely robust, with one study finding its ability to predict subsequent behaviour being second only to fMRI.[10]

Meanwhile, 'eye-tracking' involves a camera used to monitor participants' eye movements, which are measured as a reliable proxy for visual attention.[11]

Eye-tracking is a particularly useful tool for messages as it can measure whether or not a message is getting attention, which, as discussed, is vital for a message to work. It can also be used to measure what elements in a message are being attended to: for example, if you create a poster advertising a price reduction, do people even see that piece of information? Thirdly, eye-tracking can be used in conjunction with other methods to understanding *what* about a message is causing a particular reaction: for example, implicit testing may tell you that a message is being remembered, while eye-tracking can tell you this is because of the picture of a cat in a propeller hat.

Eye-tracking is ostensibly the only way to directly measure what people are paying attention to – that is, to see if people actually look at your message, or alternatively, what it is *within* your message they are looking at. However, the method can be relatively difficult and expensive to implement.

There is also a range of other – more advanced – psychological methodologies like the measurement of physiological arousal or brain activity. Although these can produce some unique and fascinating insights – with incredible power when it comes to predicting real-world behaviour[10] – they are generally costly and difficult to carry out. It is certainly advisable, however, that the serious comms professional start to test these methods and integrate them into his or her arsenal.

While non-conscious methodologies are more reliable than traditional methods like surveys or focus groups, since the latter neglect non-conscious processes, decision-making does in fact involve both conscious and non-conscious thinking, and for this reason, research suggests that the best predictive power actually comes from *combining* both types of measure.[12]

Ultimately though, it's about choosing the best tool for the job from the whole toolkit.

FOUR STEPS TO FOLLOW WHEN TESTING A MESSAGE

1 What is my goal?

Firstly, you need to think about what your desired outcome is for the message. Most of the time it will be some sort of behaviour, like an increase in sales or donations, an increase in website traffic, or a reduction in the number of people littering. However, sometimes the goal may be more abstract, like inducing more positive perceptions of salad. What change do you want your message to achieve?

▶

2 How can I achieve it?

Next, you must consider how this goal is to be achieved using the principles outlined in this book. For example, if you want to make an email more effective, you may want to test the effect of putting the word 'damn' in the subject line; alternatively, you might want to see if putting a kitten in your dating profile picture gets it more views. What change do you want to make to affect the outcome chosen previously? This is your independent variable.

3 What method captures this?

Now you need to decide which methodology to use in order to test that changing your independent variable does in fact impact your dependent variable. How can you measure the latter? It may be as simple as product sales, website hits, or number of pieces of litter dropped per hour. For more abstract outcomes, like perceptions or emotions, it is vital to use a reliable method – this is likely something other than survey testing, which is limited.

4 How do I keep things scientific?

Finally, now that you have designed your test, you need to make sure it is scientific. For example, depending on the experimental design, you may need a control group which is identical to the experimental group except for the thing being tested. Also, you must subject the data to statistical analysis and check for statistical significance; additionally, your sample must be sufficiently big in every group. Overall, your test must be robust if the results are to mean anything.

CONCLUSION

Have a look at this chart:[1]

Measles cases per year in the US

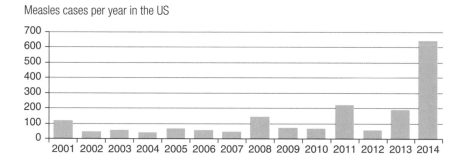

Many parents in America refuse to have their child vaccinated against measles out of fear that the measles-mumps-rubella vaccine (MMR) causes autism.

It doesn't. There has been tonnes and tonnes of reliable research showing this;[2] besides which, the original paper suggesting a link has been discredited and withdrawn, and the authoring doctor has even lost his medical licence.[3]

But here's the thing: these are very *rational* arguments.

The anti-MMR lobby, on the other hand, has the power of stickiness on its side: fear is both attention-grabbing and a very strong motivator of behaviour; the 'needles equal bad' message is a very simple one to comprehend; the lobby parades apparent case studies of autistic children who had the jab, using the power of narrative; and parents are ostensibly following the lead of their friends as well as liked and trusted celebrities like Jenny McCarthy. Dry double-blind studies have nothing on these techniques.

'We're half a chromosome away from chimpanzees and it shows.' The late majestic misanthrope Christopher Hitchens once said this,[4] and it is vital to keep in mind. The truth is, we are barely evolved monkeys: despite what we might think, our behaviour is influenced by basic and hardwired principles, which are often far more simplistic than we like to admit.

Did you know, for example, that in the month of a suicide highly publicised in the news, the national suicide rate sees a 3% increase?[5]

So, when you craft a message, you'll only get so far if you focus on persuasion and rationality. A reasoned argument for potential financial savings won't sell a price comparison site: but a meerkat with a funny accent will. If you want your message to be sticky, you'll have much more luck with 'monkey see, monkey do' than with *homo economicus.*

Now you yourself can wield the awesome power of the puppy, along with the primal, the personal and the surprising, to immediately and uncontrollably capture people's attention; you can use stories, simplicity and curiosity to get people to take on board what you're saying; and you can use memory, priming and an understanding of the human autopilot to influence people's behaviour. In short, you have everything you need to put together a message that works.

So go out there – and *get people hooked*!

EXERCISE

Supporting MMR vaccines

The anti-MMR lobby has a very sticky message, and has had a significant influence on behaviour as a result.

So far, the responses from governments have tended to target rational thinking. For example, Australian prime minister Tony Abbot announced that parents who don't immunise their children could be liable to stop receiving childcare benefits from the state[6] – though a lot of research suggests financial incentives can be poor motivators for behaviour.[7]

Using everything you've learned in this book, what would you advise the Australian government to do instead?

Firstly, design a poster advocating the MMR vaccine: what should it look like, what should be on it, and what should the copy (i.e. headline) say? Remember, you need to capture attention, get the message 'taken on board', and influencing recipients' behaviours.

Next, imagine the government is sending out letters to Australian households encouraging parents to get their children vaccinated. What *one* sentence could you add to the letter to make it more effective?

INDEX

in-store promotional materials 65, 153, 154
Indiana University 32
infants 37, 43, 52, 69–70
influencing behaviour 16–17, 112–14, 151
  direct mail 168–9
  online messages 162–3
  promotions 156–7
  workplace communications 172–3
  see also heuristics; memory; motivating behaviour; priming
infographics 162
instinct 103–4
interactive experiment 88
International Journal of Advertising 68
internet
  banner advertising 37, 65, 72, 76
  browsing behaviour 94
  cat videos 41
  food photography 34–5, 36
  global penetration 8
  memes 17–18
  mock sites 177
  novelty 67–9
  online messages 158–64
  pornography 31
  split-testing 177
  virality 18, 41, 68–9
  see also social media
interpersonal influence 170
irrational brain 20–1
isolation effect 67
ITPRA (Imagination, Tension, Prediction, Reaction and Appraisal) model 82–3
Iyengar, Sheena 25, 92–3

Jackpotjoy 71–2
John Hopkins University 69
Journal of Advertising 64–5, 93
Journal of Consumer Psychology 49
Jurassic Park (film) 176

Kahneman, Daniel 20, 120–1, 125
Kickstarter campaigns 160, 162
King's Cross station, London 65
Knorr 16
Kunz, Phillip 132

Lancaster University 142
LaPiere, Richard 10–11

laziness *see* ease
legal considerations 127
Lepper, Mark 25
Liberal Democrats 136–7
Libet, Benjamin 11
liking heuristic 134–6, 163, 169, 172–3
limbic system 22
litter 128
Loewenstein, George 83, 86
L'Oréal 57
loss aversion 6
loyalty cards 138

McDonald's 85
McVitie 42
Mailchimp 177
Malaysian Airlines 80–1
mammalian brain 22, 23, 24, 26, 44, 94
Marketing magazine 57, 118
Marks & Spencer 15
Mars 13
mass customisation 56–9
meaning, narrative 105–7
measles-mumps-rubella vaccine (MMR) 181, 182
measuring outcome behaviour 177–80
meerkats 42
memes 17–18
memory 16–17, 115–22, 151
  and attention 77, 116
  and cognitive processing 77, 116
  half-life 113
  mnemonic link system 106
  and narrative 102, 104–5, 106–7
  online messages 162
  peak-end rule 120–1
  primacy and recency 119–20
  promotions 156
  repetition 17, 116–18, 172
  Spreading Activation Theory 25, 77–8
Mercedes-Benz 68–9
mere agreement effect 139
mere-exposure effect 55
message processing *see* cognitive processing
metaphors 86–8
Milgram, Stanley 127–8, 129–30
mirror neurons 102
MMR *see* measles-mumps-rubella vaccine (MMR)